BY CURTIS STONE

Good Food, Good Life

What's for Dinner?

Relaxed Cooking with Curtis Stone

Cooking with Curtis

Surfing the Menu Again

Surfing the Menu

Good Food, Good Life

Good Food, Good Life

———

130 SIMPLE RECIPES
YOU'LL LOVE TO MAKE AND EAT

CURTIS STONE

appetite
by RANDOM HOUSE

Appetite by Random House® and
colophon are registered trademarks of Random House of Canada Limited
Published by arrangement with Ballantine Books, New York

Library and Archives of Canada Cataloguing in Publication is available upon request

ISBN: 978-0-449-01589-6
eBook ISBN: 978-0-449-01590-2

Photographs copyright © Ray Kachatorian

Book design by Liz Cosgrove

Printed and bound in China

Published in Canada by
Appetite by Random House®
a division of Random House of Canada Limited,
a Penguin Random House Company

www.penguinrandomhouse.ca

10 9 8 7 6 5 4 3 2 1

appetite
by RANDOM HOUSE

Penguin
Random
House

I would like to dedicate this book to my son and chief recipe taster, Hudson.

In only three years you have taught me so much about food and life.

Thanks, mate.

Contents

————

Introduction

————

I MAY BE STATING THE OBVIOUS HERE BUT I'LL SAY
it anyway—my life wholly and completely revolves around food. Not just
the eating of it (though my mum used to call me a greedy little monster, and
she was right—and things have never really changed), but the entire experience
that encircles food. For me, that's anything from planting and plucking up veggies in my garden with the California sun on my back to the pride that comes
with pulling a simple roast chicken out of the oven and unveiling its perfectly
golden brown skin. It's also cooking breakfast with my three-year-old son,
Hudson "Hudzini," who has more fun in the kitchen than he does playing a
game of trains, or seeing guests' faces light up when they're presented with a
unique tasting plate at my restaurant, Maude. The simple and sometimes extraordinary joys that good food brings to me makes for a very good life.

Food has made all of my dreams come true. I've been fortunate enough to
travel and cook with some of the best chefs in the world, and it's provided me
with a career that keeps me steadily on my toes, just the way I like it! I get to
host food shows and events, develop hundreds of recipes for home cooks in my
test kitchen, and spend as much time as I can cooking at my intimate twenty-
five-seat restaurant in Los Angeles. But when I really hone in on what it is I love
most about food, it's the really simple stuff like sitting around a dinner table
sharing stories and celebrating occasions over really delicious home-cooked
food, while showing a little love to the special people in my world.

I wrote *Good Food, Good Life* because I believe in just that: through tasty,
well-cooked food prepared with fresh, quality, and seasonal produce you can
have an incredible life. Good food and a fulfilled life become easier to obtain
when you've got some inspiration and encouragement to spur you on; my

hope is that you reap a good dose of both from a bunch of the recipes, tips, and experiences shared in this book.

The recipes that make up this collection are the same delicious ones that I cook at home from morning to night and include snacks, sweets, light meals, sides, drinks, breakfast, and dinner, too. There's the green juice that Hud and I make most mornings with freshly picked fruits and veggies, grilled spicy lemongrass chicken wings for a Saturday afternoon snack around the pool, "bad for me but tastes so flipping good" divine chocolate brownies that I eat much too often—plus 127 more that you'll love to make and eat.

Different stages of my life have influenced this assorted collection of dishes. For instance, I know you'll fall for the Chocolate Salted Caramel Kisses that I used to eat in the schoolyard all those years ago, and I'm excited to share some recipes that I've cooked time and again in my restaurants, such as Sesame Shrimp Toast, but have now been appropriated for the home kitchen. I mastered the art of making these babies at nineteen years of age working as an apprentice in Melbourne, Australia, and this version is so so simple for cooks of all levels to replicate.

I'm now husband to the love of my life, Lindsay, and lucky father to our two gorgeous kids. As chef of the house, I do my best to fill their bellies with as much joy and goodness as I can. Hence, there are a few of our secret family recipes divulged in each chapter, even a scaled-back cupcake interpretation of the carrot cake with brown sugar cream cheese frosting that I whipped up for Linds on our wedding day. I promise you the cupcakes are much easier to bake than our three-tiered wedding cake, and are equally delicious.

I have my beautiful family and good friends to thank for giving me a great life. I want to provide for them, nurture them, and make them deliriously happy, and the way I know how to do this is through good food.

Food has been so good to me. *Good Food, Good Life* is a celebration of all the dishes that bring overwhelming happiness to me and to the most important people in my world. I hope they'll bring just as much to you and yours.

Good Food, Good Life

Chapter 1
LIGHT MEALS

———

CAN THINK OF NO BETTER WAY to spend my time than sharing a home-cooked meal with family and good mates. The food, people, setting, time of day, music played, and cocktails mixed make every gathering an occasion. However, I do like to kick back on the couch every now and then, and tuck into a well-made sandwich or satisfying salad. Whether it's a light flatbread sandwich stuffed with summer's crispest cucumbers and sweetest tomatoes or a frisée and apple salad in the fall, there's something about eating barefoot and almost horizontal on the sofa that feels particularly indulgent.

The soups, salads, and sandwiches in this chapter are perfect for an impromptu sofa snack or quick lunch. I also like to mix 'n' match a couple to create a larger casual meal. And they're great for "cheating dinners" too. I'm a big dinner guy; I love my roast chickens, pork shoulders, and lamb ragùs (look out for these bad boys in the Dinners chapter), but occasionally I "cheat" on them and go with light 'n' delicious when the night calls for it. After a day rushing between the office and a meeting, and finishing off on the line at the restaurant, sometimes all I want to do is reheat a homemade soup, reawakening all of those yummy fresh flavors. Most of the soups included here can be made at least a day ahead. Humble and healthful soups like chicken or navy bean and ham are our go-to for chilly weeknights, but you'll find that many of the soups and a lot of the salads and sandwiches have something extra—like the luscious, thick texture and holiday flavors in the Creamy Celery Root Soup or the medley of colorful ingredients and the cilantro dressing in the Baja Salad—making them ideal for casual dinner parties too.

Roasted Beet and Quinoa Salad with Goat Cheese, Fennel, and Pecans

The tarragon vinaigrette used here coats and clings to the grains of quinoa, infusing them with plenty of tangy flavor. I love the way the pecans interplay with the nuttiness of the grain. Farro, spelt, bulgur, and even wild or brown rice also work nicely in this salad.

1. To roast the beets, preheat the oven to 350°F.

2. Place the beets in a roasting pan or baking dish, rub them with 1 tablespoon of the oil, and sprinkle with salt and pepper. Cover the pan tightly with foil and roast the beets for about 1 hour, or until they are just tender. Cool slightly.

3. Meanwhile, to cook the quinoa, heat the remaining tablespoon of oil in a medium saucepan over medium-high heat. Add the quinoa and cook, stirring, for about 3 minutes, or until the quinoa is toasted. Add 1⅔ cups water and bring to a boil. Cover the pan, reduce the heat to medium-low, and simmer for about 20 minutes, or until the quinoa has absorbed the liquid and is tender. Turn off the heat, uncover the pan, and cool completely.

4. When the beets are cool enough to handle, using a towel, rub off the skin. Cut each beet into 6 wedges and place in a medium bowl.

5. To make the vinaigrette, in a small bowl, whisk the vinegar, shallots, oil, and tarragon to blend. Season the vinaigrette to taste with salt and pepper. Add 3 tablespoons of the vinaigrette to the cooked beets and toss to coat. Let stand for 30 minutes.

6. In a large bowl, toss the arugula and fennel with enough of the vinaigrette to coat lightly. Season with salt.

7. Mound the quinoa on a platter. Top with the arugula and fennel and then with the beets. Scatter the pecans over the salad and crumble the cheese over it. Drizzle with the remaining vinaigrette and serve immediately.

SERVES: 6

PREP TIME: 15 minutes

COOK TIME: 1 hour

MAKE-AHEAD: The beets and quinoa can be cooked up to 1 day ahead, covered separately, and refrigerated.

BEETS AND QUINOA

2 pounds small beets (about 2 inches in diameter), scrubbed and trimmed

2 tablespoons olive oil

Kosher salt and freshly ground black pepper

1 cup red quinoa, rinsed

SALAD AND VINAIGRETTE

3 tablespoons champagne vinegar

3 tablespoons finely chopped shallots

3 tablespoons olive oil

1 tablespoon chopped fresh tarragon

Kosher salt and freshly ground black pepper

4 cups (not packed) baby arugula

1 fennel bulb, trimmed, cored, and shaved on a vegetable slicer or mandoline

½ cup pecans, toasted and very coarsely broken

4 ounces soft goat cheese

Grilled Vegetable Salad with Curry-Yogurt Vinaigrette

SERVES: 8

PREP TIME: 15 minutes

COOK TIME: 8 minutes

MAKE-AHEAD: The vinaigrette can be made up to 1 hour ahead, covered, and refrigerated.

The tender arugula and grilled zucchini and peppers carry the curry flavors to create a comforting summer salad. For a heartier meal, serve on a bed of couscous with a couple of Grilled Lamb Chops (page 74). The yogurt vinaigrette also tastes incredible spooned over roasted heirloom curried carrots and topped with a handful of toasted pine nuts—serve as a side.

CURRY-YOGURT VINAIGRETTE

½ cup plain Greek yogurt

¼ cup finely chopped fresh mint

½ small red onion, very finely chopped (¼ cup)

1½ teaspoons grated lime zest

¼ cup fresh lime juice

1 tablespoon white wine vinegar

Kosher salt

SALAD

3 tablespoons olive oil

1 tablespoon curry powder

2 pounds medium zucchini, cut lengthwise in half

2 red bell peppers, cored, quartered, and seeded

Kosher salt

2½ cups (not packed) baby arugula

1. To make the vinaigrette, in a bowl, whisk the yogurt, mint, onion, lime zest and juice, and vinegar to blend. Season to taste with salt. Cover and refrigerate until ready to serve.

2. To make the salad, prepare a grill for high heat.

3. In a large bowl or on a large platter, mix the oil and curry powder together. Add the zucchini and bell peppers and toss and turn to coat. Season with salt and toss again. Grill the zucchini and bell peppers for about 3 minutes per side, or until just charred but still firm. Transfer the grilled vegetables to a baking sheet and set aside to cool slightly, or let cool to room temperature.

4. Cut the zucchini on a slight angle into 1-inch-wide slices. Cut the bell peppers into ½-inch-wide strips. Return the zucchini and bell peppers to the baking sheet.

5. Just before serving, scatter the arugula over the grilled vegetables and use your hands to gently toss the vegetables and arugula with enough vinaigrette to coat lightly. Season the salad to taste with salt. Transfer the salad to a platter or individual plates, spoon a little more vinaigrette around the salad, and serve immediately.

VARIATION To roast the zucchini and bell peppers in the oven, preheat the oven to 450°F. Cut the bell peppers into 2-inch pieces, then prepare the zucchini and bell peppers as in step 3 and transfer cut side down to a heavy baking sheet. Roast for about 12 minutes, or until the vegetables are just charred but still firm. Slice the zucchini but keep the bell peppers as large pieces.

Baja Salad

Just looking at this colorful salad makes me want to dust off my surfboard and hit the Baja California coast. With succulent tomatoes, pickled red onions, crispy tortilla chips, and lime juice, it packs a zing and a crunch. Enjoy it as is; top with braised or grilled pork, beef, or chicken for a more substantial meal; or serve with a side of Humble Beans (page 113).

1. To make the dressing, in a small food processor, process the cilantro, garlic, lime juice, and liquid from the pickled onions until the garlic is minced and the cilantro is finely chopped. With the machine running, slowly pour in the oil, processing until the dressing is well blended. Season with salt.

2. Just before serving, in a large wide bowl or on a platter, gently toss the romaine, cabbage, radishes, carrot, and tomatoes with enough dressing to coat. Season with salt. Drain the pickled onions and scatter them over the salad. Top with the diced avocados, Cotija, pumpkin seeds, and crumbled tortilla chips. Serve immediately.

SERVES: 6

PREP TIME: 30 minutes

MAKE-AHEAD: The dressing can be made up to 1 day ahead, covered, and refrigerated.

CILANTRO DRESSING

¼ cup packed fresh cilantro leaves

1 garlic clove

2 tablespoons fresh lime juice

2 tablespoons liquid from the Pickled Red Onions (recipe follows)

¼ cup olive oil

Kosher salt

SALAD

3 cups coarsely torn romaine lettuce heart (from 1 head)

1½ cups shaved green cabbage

4 radishes, cut into matchstick-size strips

1 carrot, cut into matchstick-size strips

1 cup cherry tomatoes, halved

Kosher salt

Pickled Red Onions (recipe follows)

2 small avocados, halved, pitted, peeled, and cut into large chunks (about 2 cups)

½ cup coarsely crumbled Cotija cheese or feta cheese

3 tablespoons toasted shelled pumpkin seeds (pepitas)

About 1½ cups Homemade Tortilla Chips (page 218), coarsely crumbled

Pickled Red Onions

Add these pickled onions to the Mulita-Style Quesadillas (page 217), as well as the Baja Salad, or anywhere you want a little tangy acidity. They can be made up to 2 weeks ahead and stored airtight in the refrigerator.

MAKES: 2 cups if using boiling onions,
1 cup or less if using sliced onions

⅓ cup fresh lime juice
¼ cup distilled white vinegar
1 teaspoon kosher salt
10 ounces small red boiling onions (about 30), peeled and halved, or 1 red onion, thinly sliced (about 1 cup)

1. If using small onions, in a medium bowl, stir the lime juice, vinegar, and salt together.

2. Add the onions to a medium saucepan of boiling water and cook for 1 minute, or until just softened. Using a slotted spoon, transfer the onions to the bowl with the lime juice mixture. Cover and refrigerate, stirring occasionally, for at least 40 minutes, or until cold. Transfer the mixture to a jar and refrigerate until ready to use.

3. If using a sliced red onion, in a small bowl, combine the sliced onion, lime juice, vinegar, and salt. Cover and refrigerate for at least 20 minutes, stirring occasionally. Transfer the mixture to a jar and refrigerate until ready to use.

Frisée and Apple Salad with Ale Vinaigrette and Rye Croûtes

SERVES: 6

PREP TIME: 15 minutes

COOK TIME: 10 minutes

MAKE-AHEAD: The salad is best when it is just made and the croûtes are still hot.

CROÛTES

3 tablespoons salted butter, at room temperature

6 ¼-inch-thick slices rye bread

¾ cup grated Gruyère cheese

SALAD

3 tablespoons finely chopped shallots

3 tablespoons sour rye ale (such as The Bruery's Sour in the Rye ale) or other sour beer

3 tablespoons white wine vinegar

2 teaspoons Dijon mustard

⅓ cup olive oil

Kosher salt and freshly ground black pepper

3 heads frisée lettuce, white parts only (about 6 cups)

1 Granny Smith apple, cored and cut into matchstick-size strips

It's safe to say that I came up with this dish when I was kicking back and enjoying a beer. I popped the cap off a bottle of rye ale that tasted sour and a bit funky, but in a really good way. With its tangy acidity and deep flavor, I had an itching suspicion that it would be good in a vinaigrette. I'm partial to The Bruery's Sour in the Rye ale, since it has a great tartness, not to mention that it's pretty darn exquisite, but choose whichever rye beer you like. Croûtes are small rustic rounds of toasted bread with a savory topping and here, I toast them with cheese quickly at a high temperature, which makes them crisp and delicate.

1. To make the croûtes, preheat the oven to 450°F.

2. Spread the butter thinly over both sides of the slices of bread and lay the bread on a baking sheet. Top each slice with 2 tablespoons of cheese and bake for about 10 minutes, or just until the bread is crisp on the outside and the cheese is bubbling.

3. Meanwhile, to make the salad, in a large bowl, whisk the shallots, ale, vinegar, and mustard to blend. Gradually whisk in the oil. Season to taste with salt and pepper. Add the frisée and apple and toss to coat. Season again with salt and pepper if necessary.

4. Divide the salad among plates and serve with the warm croûtes alongside.

Weeknight Navy Bean and Ham Soup

The butter helps caramelize the ham and sage here, giving off a mouthwatering aroma and making the soup a pleasure to cook from the start. Since the pressure cooker will soften the beans in less than half the usual time, and there's no need to presoak the beans, you can enjoy this soup any night of the week.

1. In an 8-quart pressure cooker, melt the butter over medium-high heat. Add the ham and sauté for about 3 minutes, or until golden brown. Add the onion, carrots, celery, garlic, bay leaf, and sage and sauté for about 1 minute, or until fragrant. Add the beans, water, and broth.

2. Lock the pressure cooker lid in place and bring to high pressure over high heat, about 15 minutes. Reduce the heat to medium-low to stabilize the pressure and cook for 40 minutes. Remove from the heat and allow the pressure to subside on its own, about 20 minutes.

3. Unlock the pressure cooker and remove the lid, tilting it away from you to allow the steam to escape. The beans will be very tender. For a thicker consistency, coarsely mash the bean mixture. Season the soup to taste with salt and pepper.

4. Ladle the soup into bowls, drizzle with olive oil, and serve.

VARIATION If you don't have a pressure cooker, this can be cooked in a heavy pot in the traditional manner. Soak the beans in water for at least 12 hours. Drain the beans. In a large heavy pot, melt the butter over medium-high heat. Add the ham and sauté for about 3 minutes, or until golden brown. Add the onion, carrots, celery, garlic, bay leaf, and sage and sauté for about 1 minute, or until fragrant. Add the soaked beans, water, and broth. Bring the mixture to a simmer. Simmer the beans for about 1½ hours, or until the beans are very tender. Continue as directed.

SERVES: 8 (makes 3 quarts)

PREP TIME: 10 minutes

COOK TIME: 1 hour and 15 minutes

MAKE-AHEAD: The soup can be made up to 3 days ahead, cooled, covered, and refrigerated. Rewarm, covered, over medium heat, adding more broth if necessary.

2 tablespoons (¼ stick) unsalted butter

8 ounces ¾-inch-thick sliced cooked smoked ham (such as Black Forest), torn into ¾-inch pieces

1 medium onion, chopped

2 large carrots, diced

2 large celery stalks, diced

2 garlic cloves, finely chopped

1 bay leaf

2 tablespoons chopped fresh sage

1 pound dried navy beans or other small white beans, picked over, rinsed, and drained

5 cups water

4 cups low-sodium chicken broth

Kosher salt and freshly ground black pepper

Extra-virgin olive oil, for drizzling

Homemade Chicken Soup Makes Me Feel Better

Whenever I'm feeling under the weather, I turn to this chicken soup, which is especially hearty with the addition of brown rice. While classic recipes have carrots, celery, and onions, I use veggies like kohlrabi, celery root, and turnips to add my own touch. Dunk in a slice of Grilled Cheese Toasts (page 224) if you're feeling particularly peckish.

SERVES: 8 (makes 4 quarts)

PREP TIME: 30 minutes

COOK TIME: 1½ hours

MAKE-AHEAD: The soup can be made up to 1 day ahead, cooled, covered, and refrigerated. Rewarm, covered, over medium heat, adding more broth if necessary.

1. Using a large sharp knife, cut the chicken into 8 pieces (2 drumsticks, 2 thighs, 2 wings, and 2 breasts). Reserve the carcass.

2. Place the chicken and carcass in a heavy 8-quart pot. Add the water, bay leaf, thyme, and lemon zest and bring the water to a simmer over medium-high heat, skimming off the foam that rises to the surface. Lower the heat to medium-low and simmer gently for about 45 minutes, or until the chicken is just cooked through. Using tongs, transfer the chicken pieces to a large bowl and set aside until cool enough to handle. Set the broth aside.

3. Remove the chicken meat from the bones and discard the skin, bones, and cartilage. Coarsely shred the meat into bite-size pieces.

4. Remove the herbs, lemon zest, and chicken carcass from the broth and discard. Add the onion, carrots, kohlrabi, celery root, turnip, and rice to the broth and simmer for about 22 minutes, or until the vegetables are cooked through and the rice is tender. Add the cooked chicken and simmer for 5 minutes. Season to taste with salt and pepper.

5. Stir in the lemon juice and parsley. Ladle into bowls and serve.

1 4-pound whole chicken, rinsed and excess fat trimmed

8 cups water

1 bay leaf

1 fresh thyme sprig

Zest (removed with a vegetable peeler) and juice of 1 lemon

1 medium onion, cut into large dice (about 1½ cups)

2 carrots, cut into large dice (about 1½ cups)

1 small kohlrabi, peeled and cut into large dice (about 1 cup)

1 small celery root, peeled and cut into large dice (about 2 cups)

1 white turnip, peeled and cut into large dice (about 2 cups)

¾ cup uncooked long-grain brown rice

Kosher salt and freshly ground black pepper

2 tablespoons chopped fresh flat-leaf parsley

Quick Curry Noodle Soup

SERVES: 4 (makes about 8 cups)

PREP TIME: 10 minutes

COOK TIME: 20 minutes

MAKE-AHEAD: The recipe can be made through step 2 up to 1 day ahead. Cover the marinated shrimp and coconut broth separately and refrigerate. Return the coconut broth to a simmer before proceeding.

1 shallot, coarsely chopped

2 Fresno chiles, seeded if desired (to lessen heat) and coarsely chopped

3 garlic cloves, coarsely chopped

1 lemongrass stalk, coarsely chopped

1 tablespoon chopped peeled fresh ginger

10 fresh cilantro sprigs, leaves removed from stems, stems and leaves reserved

2 tablespoons canola oil

2 cups unsweetened coconut milk

2 cups water

1 pound peeled and deveined large shrimp (16–20 per pound), halved through the back lengthwise

1 pound skinless snapper fillets, cut into 1-inch pieces

3 ounces thin rice stick noodles, soaked in hot water for 10 minutes and drained

4 kaffir lime leaves (optional), thinly sliced

1 tablespoon fish sauce

Grated zest and juice of 2 limes

Kosher salt

This brothy soup is heavy on aromatic Thai flavors like lemongrass, ginger, cilantro, and coconut milk. The kaffir lime leaves are not essential, but if you can get your hands on a bunch, they will take the dish to the next level. Freeze leftover leaves and pull them out again for your next curry.

1. In a food processor, process the shallot, chiles, garlic, lemongrass, ginger, and cilantro stems with the oil until pureed as fine as possible, stopping the machine and scraping the sides of the bowl occasionally.

2. Heat a large heavy pot over medium-high heat. Add the chile puree and sauté for about 3 minutes, or until the mixture is fragrant. Add the coconut milk and water, cover, bring to a simmer, and simmer for about 10 minutes, or until the flavors have blended.

3. Add the shrimp, snapper, noodles, lime leaves, if using, and fish sauce to the coconut broth and simmer for about 3 minutes, or until the seafood and noodles are just cooked through. Stir in the lime zest and juice. Season to taste with salt.

4. Transfer to bowls, sprinkle with the cilantro leaves, and serve immediately.

Creamy Celery Root Soup

SERVES: 6 (makes 8 cups)

PREP TIME: 10 minutes

COOK TIME: 40 minutes

MAKE-AHEAD: The soup can be made up to 1 day ahead, cooled, covered, and refrigerated. Rewarm, covered, over low heat, adding more broth if necessary.

4 tablespoons (½ stick) unsalted butter

½ cup coarsely chopped shallots

3 pounds celery root, peeled and cut into 1-inch cubes

3 cups low-sodium chicken broth

3 cups whole milk

1 cup heavy cream

4 fresh thyme sprigs

1 bay leaf

1½ teaspoons kosher salt

We call this "Thanksgiving Soup" at my house because it has all of the flavors of this American holiday in one smooth bowl. It looks unassuming because of its pale creamy color, but each spoonful is full of flavor. For a vegetarian version, switch out the chicken broth for vegetable broth.

1. In a large heavy saucepan, melt 2 tablespoons of the butter over medium heat. Add the shallots and sauté for about 2 minutes, or until translucent. Add the celery root, broth, milk, cream, 2 of the thyme sprigs, the bay leaf, and salt and bring to a gentle simmer. Reduce the heat to medium-low and simmer very gently, uncovered, stirring occasionally, for about 35 minutes, or until the celery root is tender enough to mash with a spoon. Remove from the heat and remove the sprigs of thyme and bay leaf.

2. Working in batches, using a slotted spoon, transfer the celery root and shallots to a blender (preferably a high-powered one) and blend until smooth, adding enough of the cooking liquid to form a smooth and creamy soup (you may not need all of the liquid); return the pureed soup to the pot and rewarm over low heat before serving.

3. Just before serving, in a small skillet over medium heat, swirl the remaining 2 tablespoons butter for about 3 minutes, or until it is melted and golden brown. Remove from the heat.

4. Ladle the soup into bowls. Pluck the leaves off the remaining 2 thyme sprigs and sprinkle the leaves over the soup. Drizzle with the browned butter and serve.

Posole

Posole is a Mexican stew made with pork and hominy in a rich, flavorful broth. A pressure cooker cooks the pork quickly, intensifies its flavor, and makes it meltingly tender. However, you can just as easily simmer it away in a heavy pot for a few hours if you prefer. Everyone can enjoy customizing their bowls with the assortment of accompaniments.

1. Heat an 8-quart pressure cooker over medium-high heat. Add the oil, then add the onion, two-thirds of the chopped garlic, and the oregano and sauté for about 2 minutes, or until fragrant. Add the pork, broth, and 2 teaspoons of the salt.

2. Lock the pressure cooker lid in place and bring to high pressure over high heat, about 15 minutes. Reduce the heat to medium to stabilize the pressure and cook for 20 minutes. Remove from the heat and allow the pressure to subside on its own, about 20 minutes.

3. Meanwhile, heat a large heavy skillet over medium heat. Working in batches, toast the chiles in the skillet for about 30 seconds (be careful not to burn them, or the sauce will be bitter), or until fragrant. Transfer the toasted chiles to a large bowl and pour the hot water over them. Soak the chiles, turning occasionally, for about 20 minutes, or until softened.

4. Transfer the chiles and soaking liquid to a blender, add the remaining chopped garlic and remaining 1 teaspoon salt and puree until smooth. Set the chile sauce aside.

5. Unlock the pressure cooker and remove the lid, tilting it away from you to allow the steam to escape. Spoon off any scum and oil from the top of the stew.

6. Add the chile sauce, hominy, and cilantro to the stew and simmer for about 10 minutes to allow the flavors to blend. Ladle the stew into bowls and serve with the accompaniments.

(continued)

SERVES: 10 (makes about 4 quarts)

PREP TIME: 10 minutes, plus 20 minutes for soaking the chiles

COOK TIME: 1 hour

MAKE-AHEAD: The chile sauce can be made up to 2 days ahead, covered, and refrigerated.

1 tablespoon canola oil

1 large white onion, chopped

6 garlic cloves, chopped

1½ teaspoons dried oregano, crushed

4 pounds boneless pork shoulder, well trimmed and cut into 2-inch chunks

8 cups low-sodium chicken broth

1 tablespoon kosher salt

6 dried red New Mexico chiles (about 2 ounces total), stemmed and seeded

3 dried chiles de árbol, stemmed and seeded

1½ cups hot water

4 cups canned hominy, drained and rinsed

½ cup coarsely chopped fresh cilantro

ACCOMPANIMENTS

3 avocados, halved, pitted, peeled, and cubed

½ head green cabbage, shredded

1 medium white onion, finely diced

3 radishes, thinly sliced

4 limes, cut into wedges

2 jalapeño peppers, thinly sliced

Homemade Tortilla Chips (page 218) or warm corn tortillas

VARIATION If you don't have a pressure cooker, the posole can be cooked in a heavy pot in the traditional manner. Heat a large heavy pot over medium-high heat. Add the oil, then the onion, two-thirds of the chopped garlic, and the oregano, and sauté for about 2 minutes, or until fragrant. Add the pork, broth, and 2 teaspoons of the salt. Bring the mixture to a simmer. Simmer for 1½ hours, or until the pork is tender. Spoon off any scum and oil from the top of the stew. Continue as directed in steps 3, 4, and 6.

HOMEMADE CHILE SAUCE

Don't be afraid of making your own chile sauce, like the one here—it sure beats the stuff from a can or jar. It may taste exotic and wonderful, but it is about the easiest sauce to make: It's just a quick toasting and soaking of chiles, then a whirl in the blender with garlic and salt. Use it for enchiladas, braised meats, or even as a dip for corn chips. For the posole, I use New Mexico chiles, which are long, brick-colored dried chiles, along with little chiles de árbol for heat. Look for them in cellophane bags at most supermarkets.

Seafood Stew with Cream and Fennel

SERVES: 6

PREP TIME: 10 minutes

COOK TIME: 40 minutes

MAKE-AHEAD: The broth (without the shellfish) can be made up to 1 day ahead, cooled, covered, and refrigerated. Bring to a simmer before proceeding.

3 tablespoons unsalted butter

1 onion, thinly sliced

2 celery stalks, cut into large dice

1 fennel bulb, trimmed, fronds reserved for garnish, and bulb thinly sliced

5 garlic cloves, finely chopped

2 teaspoons coarsely chopped fresh rosemary

2 teaspoons coarsely chopped fresh thyme

1 teaspoon freshly ground black pepper

½ teaspoon red pepper flakes

¼ teaspoon fennel seeds, coarsely crushed

1 bay leaf

1 cup dry white wine

3 cups low-sodium chicken broth

3 cups water

2 cups heavy cream

1 pound halibut fillets, cut into 1½- to 2-inch pieces

Kosher salt and freshly ground black pepper

1 pound mussels, scrubbed and debearded

1 pound small Manila clams (about 36), scrubbed

For a truly special occasion, replace some of the mussels and clams with lobster and crabmeat. Serve the stew with lots of bread for soaking up every drop of the broth.

1. In a heavy 8-quart pot, melt the butter over medium heat. Add the onion, celery, fennel, garlic, rosemary, thyme, black pepper, red pepper flakes, fennel seeds, and bay leaf and sauté for about 10 minutes, or until the vegetables soften. Add the wine and simmer for about 2 minutes, or until reduced by one-fourth. Add the broth and water, bring to a simmer, and simmer for about 20 minutes, or until the flavors have blended.

2. Stir the cream into the broth, bring to a simmer, and simmer for 5 minutes.

3. Season the halibut with salt and pepper. Add the halibut, mussels, and clams to the simmering broth and simmer for about 5 minutes, or until the clams and mussels have opened and the halibut is just cooked through and opaque.

4. Divide the soup among bowls, garnish with the reserved fennel fronds, and serve.

Roast Chicken Sandwich with Giardiniera

Mother Nature and her bounty of seasonal produce are my biggest inspiration in the kitchen, but leftovers can be a great source of motivation too. Here I transform last night's dinner into lunch by sandwiching leftover roast chicken, crispy lettuce, and giardiniera (piquant pickled veggies) between two slices of soft bread. If you want to go the extra mile, add a slice or two of Gruyère, Fontina, or Asiago to your "sanga" and grill it so the cheese oozes all over the filling. Leftover roast turkey and grilled steak also work well in this sandwich.

SERVES: 4

PREP TIME: 10 minutes

COOK TIME: 10 minutes

MAKE-AHEAD: The giardiniera relish can be made up to 4 days ahead, covered, and refrigerated.

½ Simple Roast Chicken (see page 48) or store-bought rotisserie chicken

1 16-ounce jar giardiniera, drained

¼ cup fresh flat-leaf parsley leaves

1 tablespoon olive oil

¼ cup Aïoli (recipe follows)

8 ¾-inch-thick slices semolina twist bread or French bread, toasted if desired

1 cup sliced romaine lettuce leaves

1. Using your hands, pull the meat from the chicken carcass, tearing it into bite-size pieces, and set aside. Discard the bones and cartilage.

2. Rinse the giardiniera and drain well on paper towels. In a food processor, pulse the giardiniera, parsley, and oil until the giardiniera is coarsely chopped.

3. Spread the giardiniera mixture and aïoli over the bread slices. Top 4 of the slices with the lettuce and chicken, then top with the remaining bread slices. Cut the sandwiches in half and serve.

Aïoli

This garlicky mayonnaise is a lively traditional Provençal condiment that can be dolloped on burgers, spread on sliced baguettes for sandwiches, served with grilled vegetables or crispy potatoes—the list goes on. Aïoli will keep for up to 5 days, covered, and refrigerated.

MAKES: 2 cups

2 small garlic cloves
2 tablespoons Dijon mustard
¼ cup fresh lemon juice
2 large egg yolks
1 cup grapeseed oil
½ cup olive oil (not extra-virgin)
Kosher salt

1. In a food processor, combine the garlic, Dijon, lemon juice, and egg yolks and process until smooth.

2. With the motor running, slowly add the oils, processing until the mixture is emulsified and creamy. Add enough water to thin the aïoli to the desired consistency. Season to taste with salt.

Pan Bagnat

Pronounced "pahn-bahn-yah," the ingredients in this Niçoise-style sandwich are a good match for soft, crusty ciabatta bread, but a French baguette that is not dense and chewy will do the trick too. Use good-quality tuna packed in oil, not water, or sub in chunks of freshly grilled tuna from my Grilled Tuna with Rémoulade Sauce (page 86). This is, for the most part, a classic make-ahead sandwich—traditionally, it is allowed time to marinate before serving—but if you're hungry and can't wait, it's just as delicious served straightaway.

SERVES: 4

PREP TIME: 15 minutes

MAKE-AHEAD: The sandwich can be made up to 2 hours ahead, wrapped in plastic, and refrigerated, to allow the flavors to marry.

½ cup Aïoli (page 30)

¼ cup crème fraîche or sour cream

½ cup fresh basil leaves, torn

Grated zest and juice of 2 lemons

Kosher salt and freshly ground black pepper

2 5-ounce cans tuna packed in olive oil, drained

¼ cup pitted kalamata olives, coarsely chopped

2 tablespoons capers, drained and chopped

1 14-ounce loaf ciabatta bread, split horizontally

2 cups (not packed) arugula leaves

1 cup torn radicchio leaves

4 hard-boiled eggs, sliced

2 small Persian cucumbers or ½ English (hothouse) cucumber, thinly sliced lengthwise

½ red onion, thinly sliced

1. In a food processor, combine the aïoli, crème fraîche, basil, and half the lemon zest and juice and process for about 20 seconds, or until the basil is coarsely chopped but not pureed. Season the basil mayonnaise to taste with salt and pepper.

2. In a small bowl, gently fold the tuna, olives, capers, and the remaining lemon zest and juice to combine, keeping the tuna in large chunks as much as possible.

3. Lay the ciabatta cut side up on a cutting board and spread the basil mayonnaise over both pieces. Scatter the arugula and radicchio over the bottom piece. Lay the slices of egg atop the lettuces and follow with the tuna mixture, cucumbers, and onion. Top with the other piece of bread.

4. Cut into 4 sandwiches and serve.

Veggie Flatbread Sandwich with Feta-Yogurt Spread

The cool flavors of cucumber, lemon, and mint make this sandwich a great choice for a light lunch in the summertime, and the tangy feta cheese provides a nice bite. For added protein, I throw in a sliced hard-boiled egg or leftover grilled chicken or lamb.

SERVES: 4

PREP TIME: 10 minutes

COOK TIME: 5 minutes

MAKE-AHEAD: The feta-yogurt spread can be made up to 5 days ahead, covered, and refrigerated.

6 ounces feta cheese

½ cup plain Greek yogurt

Kosher salt and freshly ground black pepper

Grilled Flatbreads with Garlic-Rosemary Oil (page 230) or 4 purchased naan, warmed

¼ English (hothouse) cucumber, thinly sliced

½ small red onion, thinly sliced

1 avocado, halved, pitted, peeled, and sliced

1 tomato, sliced

⅓ cup fresh mint leaves, coarsely torn

1 lemon

1. In a food processor, combine the feta and yogurt and process until smooth and creamy. Season to taste with salt and pepper.

2. Spread the feta-yogurt mixture over the flatbreads. Arrange the cucumber, onion, avocado, and tomato slices over one half of each bread. Season with salt and pepper. Top with the mint. Finely grate some lemon zest over the filling and then halve the lemon and squeeze some juice over. Fold the bread over the filling, cut the sandwiches in half if desired, and serve.

Pork Burger with
Spicy Ginger Pickles

You're not gonna find this Hawaiian-style burger, with kimchi mayonnaise and ginger pickles, on any drive-thru menu. Mix up a little extra kimchi mayo for a flavorful dipping sauce if you're serving the burgers with fries.

SERVES: 4

PREP TIME: 15 minutes

COOK TIME: 10 minutes

MAKE-AHEAD: The burger patties can be formed up to 4 hours ahead, covered, and refrigerated.

1. Prepare a grill for medium-high heat.

2. In a medium bowl, mix the scallions, ginger, garlic, red pepper flakes, and sesame oil.

3. In a large bowl, mix the pork with 2 tablespoons of the ginger-garlic mixture. Form the mixture into 4 patties that are slightly larger than the buns.

4. Whisk the brown sugar and soy sauce into the remaining ginger-garlic mixture; set aside. In a small bowl, mix the kimchi and aïoli. Season to taste with salt and set aside.

5. Grill the patties for 3 to 4 minutes, or until grill marks form on the first side. Turn the patties over, generously brush with some of the soy sauce mixture, and continue grilling for 3 to 4 more minutes, or until the patties are cooked through but still juicy.

6. Meanwhile, lightly oil the cut sides of the buns with the canola oil and grill the buns, cut side down, for about 2 minutes, or until they are toasted and grill marks have formed.

7. Spread the kimchi mayonnaise over the bun bottoms. Top with the patties, then generously brush more of the soy sauce mixture over the patties. Divide the pickles among the burgers and top with the cilantro sprigs. Cover with the bun tops and serve.

2 scallions, trimmed and thinly sliced

1¾-inch piece fresh ginger, peeled and grated

1 garlic clove, finely chopped

Pinch of red pepper flakes

1 teaspoon toasted sesame oil

1 pound freshly ground pork (not lean)

¼ cup packed light brown sugar

¼ cup soy sauce

⅓ cup kimchi, drained and finely chopped

⅓ cup Aïoli (page 30) or purchased mayonnaise

Kosher salt

4 hamburger buns, split

1 tablespoon canola oil

Spicy Ginger Pickles (recipe follows)

1 cup (not packed) cilantro sprigs

Spicy Ginger Pickles

Add heat to your cucumbers by pickling them with jalapeño and ginger. These pickles taste great in burgers and sandwiches or finely diced and folded into potato salad. They'll keep for up to 2 weeks, stored airtight in the refrigerator.

MAKES: about 3 cups

1½ cups rice vinegar
1½ cups water
¼ cup sugar
4 teaspoons kosher salt
½ English (hothouse) cucumber, thinly sliced
1 small white onion, thinly sliced into rounds
1 jalapeño pepper, thinly sliced
2 teaspoons finely chopped peeled fresh ginger

1. In a small saucepan, combine the vinegar, water, sugar, and salt and bring to a boil over medium-high heat, stirring until the sugar and salt dissolve.

2. In a medium nonreactive (glass, stainless steel, or ceramic) bowl, combine the cucumber, onion, jalapeño, and ginger. Pour the vinegar mixture over the cucumber mixture and gently press to help submerge it. As the mixture cools, the vegetables will soften and become completely submerged. Refrigerate, uncovered, for at least 1 hour, or until completely cool, before serving.

Chapter 2
DINNERS

———

Grilled Lamb Chops with Kalamata Salsa Verde 74

Herb-Crusted Rack of Lamb with Fennel 77

Stracci with Braised Lamb Ragù 78

Roasted Salmon and Beets with Herb Vinaigrette 82

Maple-Glazed Planked Salmon 85

Grilled Tuna with Rémoulade Sauce 86

Whole Grilled Branzino with Soy-Ginger Sauce 89

Grilled Crab Legs with Avocado Chimichurri 90

Risotto with Shrimp, Arugula, and Lemon Cream 93

Almond Falafel 94

Winter Vegetable Curry with Chile-Mint Chutney 98

Potato and Zucchini Enchiladas with Habanero Salsa 101

Spaghettini with Lemon and Ricotta 104

DINNER IS THE REIGNING MEAL, THE grand finale, of each day. I take comfort in knowing that I get to go home after a day on set or in the test kitchen to decompress over dinner with my family or, once or twice a week, with a couple of friends.

I truly believe that the promise of good food sets the scene for special moments. It begins with the simple joys of cooking, like when onions and garlic hit the pan and release their aromas, drawing my family to the kitchen to ask, "Sooo, what's cooking?" or when the meat drops into the skillet, letting off a fierce hiss and sizzle—a signal to guests that something delicious is on the way. And it finishes with us tucking into the food, with our eyes lighting up over the sweetness of the summer tomatoes in the Chicken with Ranchera Salsa, or slurping up the silky-smooth Spaghettini with Lemon and Ricotta, getting so involved in the food that we forget all about conversation—just for a minute or two.

I know it's not always easy to get dinner on the table after a mad day, but being able to enjoy this intimate experience with the special people in our lives makes it worth going to the effort to prepare a homemade meal as often as we can. I've shared twenty-eight recipes in this chapter to inspire dinners for many years to come. They range from weeknight dishes that can be ready in thirty minutes or less, like the Chicken and Broccoli Casserole, to Porcini-Braised Beef with Horseradish Mascarpone, which simmers away for five hours, making it perfect for Sunday, when you can revel in its rich smell all afternoon. And vegetarians and meat eaters alike will be pleased with the four meat-free recipes that pay homage to just how good seasonal veggies can be when cooked properly, with an emphasis on interesting, bold flavor combos.

The day is done; let's eat.

Piri Piri Chicken with Slaw

Piri piri is a Portuguese sauce that combines garlic, chiles, red wine vinegar, and oil. While I like things spicy, the level of heat in this pureed sauce can be adjusted if you like; just use fewer Thai chiles for a milder ride. But do keep in mind that the accompanying slaw and flatbreads help to offset the heat. The slaw is also a great side dish for seafood and other meats—try it with Maple-Glazed Planked Salmon (page 85) or sausages.

1. To prepare the piri piri chicken, in a food processor, blend the chiles, garlic, vinegar, and salt until smooth. With the machine running, gradually add the oil.

2. In a large bowl, toss the chicken with ⅔ cup of the piri piri mixture to coat. Cover and refrigerate for at least 30 minutes, and up to 1 day. Refrigerate the remaining piri piri sauce.

3. Prepare a grill for high heat. Thread the chicken pieces onto skewers. Grill the skewers, turning frequently and basting with ⅓ cup of the remaining piri piri sauce, for about 12 minutes, or until the chicken is cooked through and charred in spots.

4. Meanwhile, to make the slaw, in a large bowl, combine the cabbage, cucumber, onion, and mint. In a small bowl, whisk the lime zest and juice with the oil to blend. Toss the cabbage mixture with enough dressing to coat. Season to taste with salt.

5. To serve, divide the chicken skewers, slaw, and flatbreads among four plates. Serve the remaining piri piri sauce alongside.

SERVES: 4

PREP TIME: 20 minutes, plus 30 minutes to marinate the chicken

COOK TIME: 12 minutes

MAKE-AHEAD: The chicken can be marinated for up to 1 day.

CHICKEN

6 large red Fresno chiles (about 5 ounces), coarsely chopped

4 red Thai chiles, stemmed

5 garlic cloves

¼ cup red wine vinegar

2½ teaspoons kosher salt

⅔ cup olive oil

1 pound boneless, skinless chicken thighs, cut into 2 to 3 pieces each

Bamboo skewers, soaked in water for at least 1 hour, or metal skewers

SLAW

¼ small head green cabbage, very thinly sliced (about 2½ cups)

¼ English (hothouse) cucumber, halved lengthwise and thinly sliced

¼ white onion, very thinly sliced

¼ cup loosely packed fresh mint leaves, thinly sliced

1 tablespoon finely grated lime zest

2 tablespoons fresh lime juice

2 tablespoons extra-virgin olive oil

Kosher salt

Grilled Flatbreads with Garlic-Rosemary Oil (page 230) or 4 purchased naan

Simple Roast Chicken
and Potatoes

SERVES: 4

PREP TIME: 10 minutes

COOK TIME: 55 minutes

1 4-pound whole chicken, legs tied together

3 tablespoons grapeseed oil

Kosher salt and freshly ground black pepper

8 small Yukon gold potatoes (about
4 ounces each), halved

1 tablespoon all-purpose flour

¾ cup reduced-sodium chicken broth

This mouthwatering bird is a classic, and every family has their favorite version. Well, here's mine, which is made with just a few ingredients but has served my family and me very well over the years. Follow this recipe for a golden bird with juicy meat and some of the tastiest potatoes you could hope for. Stick with small Yukons—they are the perfect size and their waxy skins become nice and crunchy. Leftover chicken can be stored airtight in the refrigerator for up to two days and used for sandwiches (see page 29), salads, or soups.

1. Position a rack in the center of the oven and preheat the oven to 425°F.

2. Place the chicken on a large heavy rimmed baking sheet. Rub 2 tablespoons of the oil all over the chicken and season it generously with salt and pepper.

3. In a medium bowl, toss the potatoes with the remaining 1 tablespoon oil to coat. Season the potatoes with salt and pepper and place them around the chicken.

4. Roast for 55 minutes, or until the thickest part of the chicken thighs all reach 160°F and the juices run clear when pierced and the potatoes are tender but crisp on the outside. Transfer the chicken and potatoes to a platter and let rest for 10 minutes before serving.

5. Meanwhile, pour the pan drippings into a small liquid measuring cup. Spoon off the fat from the drippings, reserving 1 tablespoon of the fat. In a small heavy saucepan, heat the reserved fat over medium-high heat. Whisk in the flour. Continue whisking for about 1 minute to cook the flour. Whisk in the pan drippings, broth, and any juices that have accumulated on the platter. Simmer, whisking, for about 2 minutes, or until the gravy thickens slightly. Season to taste with salt and pepper.

6. Serve the chicken and potatoes immediately with the gravy.

Chicken with Ranchera Salsa

SERVES: 4

PREP TIME: 10 minutes

COOK TIME: 18 minutes

MAKE-AHEAD: The ingredients for the ranchera salsa can be prepped up to 4 hours ahead, covered in the baking dish, and refrigerated until ready to broil.

1½ pounds heirloom tomatoes, cut into large cubes

1 small white onion, finely diced (1 cup)

⅓ cup chopped fresh cilantro, plus ½ cup leaves for garnish

2 jalapeño peppers, seeded if desired (for less heat) and finely chopped

3 garlic cloves, finely chopped

2 tablespoons plus 1 teaspoon extra-virgin olive oil

Kosher salt

4 boneless, skinless chicken breasts (about 1½ pounds)

1 cup grated pepper Jack cheese (about 4 ounces)

¼ cup crumbled queso fresco or feta cheese

Here diced heirloom tomatoes, onion, garlic, and chiles are broiled in the baking dish to make a ranchera sauce for the chicken breasts. It's a one-pan wonder to be served straight from the baking dish, along with a green salad or Humble Beans (page 113), and warm corn tortillas for scooping up the sauce.

1. Preheat the broiler. In a 13 x 9 x 2-inch baking dish, toss the tomatoes, onion, chopped cilantro, jalapeños, and garlic with 2 tablespoons of the oil. Season with salt. Broil for about 3 minutes, or until the vegetables begin to soften and char. Remove from the broiler and stir the vegetables.

2. In a medium bowl, sprinkle the chicken with salt and the remaining 1 teaspoon oil and toss to coat. Nestle the chicken into the tomato mixture and turn to coat. Broil for about 12 minutes, or until the chicken is cooked through and the sauce is bubbling and slightly charred on top.

3. Sprinkle the cheeses over the chicken. Broil for 2 to 3 minutes, or until the cheese melts and begins to brown. Sprinkle with the cilantro leaves and serve.

Chicken and Broccoli Casserole

A casserole with a bubbling sauce and golden topping is the very definition of a homey family dinner, but it's also a great dish to serve to a group of buddies. My update is to make it with all fresh ingredients. Who can resist morsels of juicy chicken, meaty bits of mushrooms, and broccoli florets bathed in gravy, with a crunchy Parm and bread crumb topping? Not me, or anyone in my house. (See photograph on page 40.)

SERVES: 4 to 6

PREP TIME: 20 minutes

COOK TIME: 20 minutes

MAKE-AHEAD: The chicken-broccoli mixture can be made up to 1 day ahead, covered and refrigerated. To rewarm, cover the baking dish with foil and bake at 350°F for about 20 minutes, or until hot, then top with the bread crumb mixture and broil as directed.

6 boneless, skinless chicken thighs (about 1½ pounds), cut into large bite-size pieces

Kosher salt and freshly ground black pepper

3 tablespoons canola oil

8 ounces white mushrooms, thickly sliced

¾ cup finely chopped onion

2 garlic cloves, finely chopped

2 teaspoons chopped fresh thyme

¼ cup dry white wine

1½ tablespoons all-purpose flour

2 cups whole milk

⅓ cup heavy cream

12 ounces broccoli, trimmed, cut into 1-inch florets with 1-inch stems, and blanched for 1 minute (see Note)

¾ cup finely grated Parmesan cheese

½ cup panko (Japanese dried bread crumbs)

1. Preheat the broiler. Season the chicken with salt and pepper. Heat a large nonstick skillet over medium-high heat. Add ½ tablespoon of the oil and the chicken and cook, turning the chicken occasionally, for about 8 minutes, or until golden. Transfer the chicken to a bowl.

2. Add ½ tablespoon of the oil and the mushrooms to the pan and sauté the mushrooms for about 4 minutes, or until golden. Add the onion, garlic, and thyme and sauté for about 2 minutes, or until the onion begins to soften. Add the wine and simmer for about 20 seconds, or until it evaporates. Sprinkle the flour over the mushrooms and stir to blend. Stir in the milk and cream and bring to a boil, then reduce the heat to medium and simmer gently, stirring, for about 3 minutes, or until the sauce thickens slightly.

3. Stir the chicken, with any accumulated juices, and the broccoli into the sauce and cook for about 3 minutes, or until the chicken and broccoli are warm. Season to taste with salt and pepper. Transfer the mixture to a 9-inch baking dish or gratin dish.

4. In a medium bowl, mix the Parmesan cheese, panko, and the remaining 1 tablespoon oil, tossing well, then sprinkle the mixture over the top of the casserole. Broil, uncovered, watching closely, for 2 to 3 minutes, or until the bread crumb mixture is golden brown.

BLANCHING BASICS

Don't be afraid of fancy culinary terms like "blanching." Basically all you're doing is cooking food, like broccoli, in boiling salted water for just a few minutes, or until its color brightens, then plunging it into ice water to stop the cooking. It's necessary in this recipe to form the delicious creamy sauce—if the broccoli is not blanched first, the sauce will curdle—so don't skip it.

Chicken Chile Verde

SERVES: 4 (makes about 8 cups)

PREP TIME: 10 minutes

COOK TIME: 1 hour

MAKE-AHEAD: The chile can be made up to 2 days ahead, cooled, covered, and refrigerated. Rewarm, covered, over medium heat.

1 4½-pound whole chicken, cut into 2 thighs, 2 drumsticks, 2 breasts, and 2 wings

Kosher salt and freshly ground black pepper

4 cups low-sodium chicken broth

1 onion, cut into large pieces

4 garlic cloves

6 tomatillos (about 1 pound total), husked and rinsed

4 jalapeño peppers, seeded and coarsely chopped

1 tablespoon olive oil

6 scallions, green tops coarsely chopped, white bottoms thinly sliced and reserved for garnish

¼ cup raw shelled pumpkin seeds (pepitas)

¾ cup loosely packed fresh cilantro leaves with tender stems

½ teaspoon cayenne pepper

½ teaspoon ground cumin

2 tablespoons fresh lime juice

GARNISHES

1 cup shredded iceberg, romaine lettuce, or green cabbage

¼ cup crumbled queso fresco

1 avocado, halved, pitted, peeled, and sliced

¼ cup fresh cilantro leaves

1 lime, cut into wedges

Although garnishes can sometimes seem like little more than an afterthought, they play a key role in this mildly spicy green chile, adding refreshing crunch from the lettuce, creaminess from the avocado and crumbled cheese, and a lift from the squeeze or two of lime.

1. Season the chicken with salt and pepper. In a large heavy pot, combine the chicken, broth, half of the onion, and 2 garlic cloves and bring the broth to a boil over medium-high heat. As the broth comes to a boil, use a spoon to remove the scum that rises to the surface. Reduce the heat, cover, and simmer gently for about 50 minutes, or until the chicken pulls apart easily. (Be sure to gently simmer the chicken, not boil it senseless, for lovely, tender meat.)

2. Meanwhile, preheat the oven to 400°F.

3. Line a baking sheet with foil. On the baking sheet, toss the tomatillos, jalapeños, the remaining onion, and the remaining 2 garlic cloves with the oil to coat. Roast for about 20 minutes, or until the vegetables are tender and beginning to caramelize. Add the scallion greens and pumpkin seeds to the baking sheet and roast for about 5 minutes, or until the pumpkin seeds are toasted.

4. Transfer the tomatillo mixture to a food processor. Add the cilantro, cayenne, cumin, and lime juice and puree until smooth. Season with salt and pepper.

5. When the chicken is tender, remove it from the broth and set aside to cool slightly. Strain the broth through a fine-mesh sieve and discard the solids. Return the broth to the pot and simmer for about 10 minutes, or until reduced by one-third.

6. Meanwhile, as soon as the chicken is cool enough to handle, remove the meat, coarsely shredding it with your hands; discard the bones, skin, and cartilage.

7. Remove the reduced broth from the heat. Stir in the shredded chicken and tomatillo puree. Bring to a simmer over medium heat, and simmer for 5 minutes to blend the flavors. Season with salt and pepper.

8. Ladle the chile into bowls. Garnish with the lettuce, queso fresco, avocado, cilantro, and reserved scallion whites. Serve with the lime wedges.

Roasted Pork Belly with Homemade Applesauce

One of my favorite family meals growing up was my mum and granny's roast pork. I like to serve the rich, tender pork belly with applesauce made with Calvados and a bit of star anise. You can also dice the meat and use it for hash or reheat on the grill and shred it for a taco filling. Buy pork belly from your local specialty butcher or Asian market.

1. Preheat the oven to 350°F.

2. Using a small sharp knife, score the fat that covers the pork belly in a crosshatch pattern. In a small bowl, mix the salt, garlic powder, and pepper to blend. Rub the spice mixture all over the pork belly, working it into the scored surface.

3. Place a wire rack on a rimmed baking sheet, set the pork belly fat side up on the rack, and cover the pork with foil. Roast for about 2 hours, or until the pork is tender.

4. Increase the heat to 400°F, remove the foil from the pork, and continue roasting for about 30 minutes, or until the pork belly is browned all over and pull-apart tender. Let rest for about 15 minutes.

5. Carve the pork and serve with the applesauce.

SERVES: 8

PREP TIME: 15 minutes

COOK TIME: 2½ hours

MAKE-AHEAD: The pork belly can be roasted up to 2 days ahead, cooled, covered, and refrigerated. To rewarm, cut the pork into portions and either sear them in a nonstick skillet over medium heat until golden brown on all sides and heated through, roast them in a 350°F oven, or grill them.

1 3-pound piece pork belly (skin removed)
1 tablespoon kosher salt
1 teaspoon garlic powder
1 teaspoon freshly ground black pepper
Homemade Applesauce (recipe follows)

GET CREATIVE

I've purposely kept my roasted pork belly simple so that you can take it in any direction you'd like. For example, for the rich intoxicating flavors of Mexican cuisine, mix 2 teaspoons each ancho chile powder and kosher salt, 1½ teaspoons ground cumin, and ½ teaspoon each freshly ground black pepper and garlic powder and rub the spice mixture over the pork belly. You'll want to dice the pork, or pull it apart, and tuck it into tacos, burritos, Mulita-Style Quesadillas (page 217), or enchiladas.

Or, for five-spice pork belly, simply coat the pork belly with 1 tablespoon five-spice powder and 2 teaspoons kosher salt. This is especially delicious in bánh mì sandwiches.

Homemade Applesauce

Pork and applesauce are a classic match, and for good reason. The tartness of the apple counteracts the richness of the pork. The applesauce can be made up to 3 days ahead, cooled, covered, and refrigerated. If desired, rewarm, covered, over medium-low heat before serving.

MAKES: 4 cups

3 tablespoons Calvados or other apple brandy
2 tablespoons (¼ stick) unsalted butter
1 tablespoon sugar
½ teaspoon kosher salt
1 whole star anise
1 whole clove
2½ pounds Fuji apples (about 5 large or 7 small), cored and cut into quarters

1. Preheat the oven to 400°F.

2. In a small heavy saucepan, stir the Calvados, butter, sugar, salt, star anise, and clove over medium heat until the butter melts.

3. In a medium bowl, toss the apples with the melted butter mixture to coat. Place the apples cut side down in a 9-inch square baking dish. Roast for about 45 minutes, or until the apples are soft. Set aside until the apples are cool enough to handle.

4. Using a spoon, scoop the flesh from the apple peels and discard the peels. Remove and discard the star anise and clove. Using a potato masher, carefully mash the apples to a chunky consistency, in the baking dish, with the juices. Serve the applesauce warm, at room temperature, or cold.

Parm-Crusted Pork Chops with Lemony Kale Salad

To retain the crumbed chops' moisture and natural tenderness, make sure you don't overcook them—they require just a few minutes in the pan. If you like, you can buy ½-inch-thick chops and forgo pounding them. But I prefer to buy thicker chops and pound them, which makes them even more tender.

1. Preheat the oven to 450°F.

2. To prepare the pork chops, place the flour in a pie plate. In a second pie plate, lightly whisk the eggs to blend. In a third pie plate, mix the panko, Parmesan cheese, and parsley.

3. Using a meat mallet, pound each pork chop between two sheets of plastic wrap to about a ½-inch thickness. Sprinkle the chops generously on both sides with salt and pepper. Dip 1 chop into the flour, turning to coat lightly, then dip into the eggs, letting the excess drip off, and then into the bread crumb mixture, patting firmly to coat completely, and place on a baking sheet lined with parchment paper. Repeat with the remaining chops. Cover and refrigerate for 30 minutes.

4. In each of two large nonstick skillets or flat griddle pans, melt 2 tablespoons of the butter with 1 tablespoon of the oil over medium heat. Add 2 chops to each pan and cook for about 3 minutes, or until golden brown on the bottom. Turn the pork chops over, add 1 tablespoon of the remaining butter and ½ tablespoon of the remaining oil to each pan, letting the butter melt around the cutlets. Cook for about 3 minutes, or until the chops are golden brown on the bottom and just cooked through. Transfer the chops to a plate lined with paper towels to absorb any excess oil and butter.

5. Meanwhile, to prepare the salad and roast the tomatoes, place the tomatoes on a heavy baking sheet, drizzle with the olive oil, and season with salt and pepper. Roast for about 5 minutes, or until the tomatoes are hot and begin to burst and char.

6. While the tomatoes roast, in a medium bowl, toss the kale with the lemon zest and juice and the extra-virgin olive oil. Season with salt and pepper.

7. Serve the pork chops with the kale salad and roasted tomatoes.

SERVES: 4

PREP TIME: 30 minutes

COOK TIME: 30 minutes

MAKE-AHEAD: The pork chops can be breaded up to 2 hours ahead, covered, and refrigerated.

PORK CHOPS

1 cup all-purpose flour

2 large eggs

1½ cups panko (Japanese dried bread crumbs)

1 cup freshly grated Parmesan cheese

¼ cup finely chopped fresh flat-leaf parsley

4 bone-in pork chops (about 8 ounces each and ¾ inch thick)

Kosher salt and freshly ground black pepper

6 tablespoons (¾ stick) unsalted butter

3 tablespoons olive oil

SALAD

4 bunches cherry tomatoes on the vine or about 20 cherry tomatoes

2 tablespoons extra-virgin olive oil

Kosher salt and freshly ground black pepper

½ bunch cavolo nero (Tuscan kale), stemmed and thinly sliced (about 4 cups)

Grated zest of 2 lemons

2 tablespoons fresh lemon juice

2 tablespoons extra-virgin olive oil

Braised Pork with Spicy Chipotle Sauce

SERVES: 6

PREP TIME: 15 minutes

COOK TIME: 8½ hours

MAKE-AHEAD: The braised pork can be made up to 2 days ahead, cooled, covered, and refrigerated. Rewarm, covered, on the high setting of the slow cooker.

SAUCE

1 28-ounce can whole tomatoes

2 tablespoons chopped canned chipotle chiles in adobo (about 3)

5 garlic cloves

1 teaspoon dried oregano

½ teaspoon ground cumin

1 cup low-sodium chicken broth

POT ROAST

1 4-pound boneless pork shoulder roast, butterflied

Kosher salt and freshly ground black pepper

All-purpose flour, for dredging

3 tablespoons canola oil

1 pound medium red-skinned potatoes (about 4), halved lengthwise

1 onion, halved and cut into 1-inch-wide strips

2 yellow bell peppers, seeded, and cut into 1-inch-wide strips

1 poblano chile, seeded and cut into 1-inch-wide strips

⅔ cup chopped fresh cilantro

Corn tortillas or flour tortillas, warmed

Serve corn or flour tortillas alongside this slow cooker pot roast so everyone can make tacos at the table or use them to mop up the flavorful chipotle sauce. Got leftovers? Shred the meat and toss with some of the sauce and vegetables, then roll up in flour tortillas for awesome burritos.

1. To make the sauce, in a blender, combine the tomatoes with their juices, the chipotle chiles, garlic, oregano, and cumin and puree until smooth. Blend in the broth. Set aside.

2. To cook the pot roast, preheat a slow cooker on the high-heat setting.

3. Sprinkle the pork generously with salt and pepper. Dredge the pork in flour to coat lightly all over. Heat a large heavy pot over medium-high heat. Add the oil and then the pork and cook, turning often, for about 10 minutes, or until the meat is browned on all sides. Transfer the pork to the slow cooker. Arrange the potatoes around the pork.

4. Pour off any excess oil from the pot. Add the onion, bell peppers, and poblano chile and sauté over medium-high heat, scraping up any browned bits on the bottom of the pot, for about 5 minutes, or until the vegetables begin to soften. Add the sauce and bring to a boil over high heat.

5. Carefully transfer the sauce and vegetables to the slow cooker. Cover and cook for 4 hours. Turn the pork over, cover, and continue cooking for 2 hours. Stir the cilantro into the slow cooker and cook for 2 more hours, or until the meat is very tender when pierced with a fork.

6. Transfer the pork to a cutting board. Skim off the excess fat from the surface of the sauce and season the sauce with salt and pepper. Slice the pork and arrange it on six plates. Spoon the vegetables and sauce over. Serve with warm tortillas.

VARIATION If desired, the pork can be braised in the traditional manner. Once the pork is brown (in step 3), transfer it to a bowl. Cook the onion, peppers, and chile as directed in step 4, then return the pork to the pot and add the potatoes. Skip step 5. Cover the pot and braise the pork in the oven at 300°F, turning it over halfway through, for 3½ hours, or until the meat is very tender. Stir in the cilantro. Continue as directed in step 6.

Spice-Rubbed Pork Tenderloin with White Barbecue Sauce and Grilled Asparagus

Back in Australia, we fire up the barbecue when we want to quickly grill some steaks or, yes, shrimp. But "barbecue" took on a whole new meaning when I started traveling around the States. It's a cooking style that's all about low and slow. Not only that, it's a cooking style with so many variations that it would take a few delicious lifetimes to devour them all. One type that I recently got into is from northern Alabama, where they serve a white mayonnaise-based sauce with their 'cue. Here I serve the sauce with succulent grilled spice-rubbed pork tenderloin. It would also be good with a beef tri-tip roast or grilled chicken.

SERVES: 6

PREP TIME: 15 minutes

COOK TIME: 15 minutes

MAKE-AHEAD: The barbecue sauce can be made up to 4 days ahead, covered, and refrigerated.

2 pork tenderloins (about 1 pound each)

3 tablespoons olive oil

2 tablespoons sweet paprika

2 teaspoons garlic powder

2 teaspoons onion powder

¾ teaspoon cayenne pepper

1 bunch asparagus, woody ends removed

Kosher salt and freshly ground black pepper

1 poblano chile

1 cup Aïoli (page 30) or mayonnaise

¼ cup cider vinegar

1 small white onion, thinly sliced into rings (about ½ cup)

½ cup loosely packed fresh flat-leaf parsley leaves

1. On a baking sheet, coat the pork tenderloins all over with 2 tablespoons of the oil. In a small bowl, mix the paprika, garlic powder, onion powder, and ½ teaspoon of the cayenne pepper. Coat the pork tenderloins all over with the spice mixture. Set aside to marinate while you prepare the grill.

2. Prepare a grill for medium-high heat.

3. On another baking sheet, toss the asparagus with the remaining 1 tablespoon oil to coat. Season with salt and pepper.

4. Grill the poblano chile, turning as needed, for about 8 minutes, or until charred all over. Transfer the chile to a small bowl, cover with plastic wrap, and set aside until cool enough to handle. Peel, seed, and dice the chile. Return the diced chile to the bowl and mix in the aïoli, vinegar, and the remaining ¼ teaspoon cayenne pepper. Season the sauce with salt and black pepper. Set aside.

5. Brush the grill grates with oil. Season the pork with salt and pepper and grill for about 8 minutes, turning every 2 minutes, or until the outside of the pork is heavily caramelized and it is cooked to an internal temperature of 150°F. Transfer to a cutting board to rest for about 10 minutes.

6. While the pork is resting, lightly oil the grill grates. Grill the asparagus, turning as needed, for about 4 minutes, or until lightly charred but still crisp-tender. Toss the grilled asparagus with the onion and parsley.

7. Slice the pork against the grain into ¼-inch-thick slices. Serve with the asparagus and sauce alongside.

Penne with Sausage and Broccoli Rabe

I can't help but go back for more (and more) of this dish; it's the perfect example of the delicious simplicity of rustic Italian fare. I often eat a big bowl topped with a healthy amount of shredded Pecorino, then slink back to the skillet where the leftovers are waiting and pick away until there is none left. You could substitute the broccoli rabe with kale—either of these dark, leafy winter greens will provide great texture, earthy flavor, and a boost of nutrients. This is a true à la minute dish; it takes just minutes to make and should be enjoyed as soon as it comes together.

SERVES: 4

PREP TIME: 5 minutes

COOK TIME: 15 minutes

4 sweet Italian sausages (about 1⅓ pounds total), casings removed

½ bunch broccoli rabe, trimmed and sliced (about 2 cups)

2 garlic cloves, chopped

½ cup dry white wine

1¼ cups tomato sauce

10 ounces penne

Kosher salt and freshly ground black pepper

2 tablespoons freshly shredded Pecorino cheese

1. Bring a large pot of salted water to a boil over high heat. Meanwhile, heat a large heavy skillet over medium-high heat. Add the sausages and cook, breaking the meat up with a wooden spoon, for about 6 minutes, or until golden brown. Add the broccoli rabe and garlic and cook for about 4 minutes, or until the broccoli rabe leaves are wilted. Add the wine and then the tomato sauce, bring to a simmer, and cook for about 3 minutes, or until the liquid is reduced by one-fourth.

2. When the water comes to a boil, add the penne and cook, stirring often so the pasta doesn't stick together, for about 8 minutes, or until tender but firm to the bite. Drain, reserving about ½ cup of the cooking water.

3. Toss the penne with the sauce, adding enough of the reserved cooking water to thin the sauce to the desired consistency. Season to taste with salt and pepper. Sprinkle with the cheese and serve immediately.

Grilled Rib-Eye Steak with Mouth-on-Fire Salsa

SERVES: 4 to 6

PREP TIME: 5 minutes

COOK TIME: 15 minutes

4 boneless rib-eye steaks (about 12 ounces each and 1 inch thick)

1 tablespoon olive oil

Kosher salt and freshly ground black pepper

Mouth-on-Fire Salsa (page 220)

SPECIAL EQUIPMENT:

3 cups hickory wood chips, soaked in cold water for 1 hour

Smoker wood chip box or a 13 x 9-inch aluminum foil pan (if using a gas grill)

After a long week at work, there's nothing quite like the feeling of grilling up a steak while sipping on a cold one and knowing that I have two free days ahead. Throw some red bell peppers and onions on the grill to serve alongside the steaks, or serve with Humble Beans (page 113). I buy big, thick steaks to achieve that juicy, rosy medium-rare doneness, but if you don't have a Fred Flinstone appetite, the leftovers make killer steak sangas.

1. Let the steaks stand at room temperature while you prepare a grill for medium-high heat: *For a gas grill*, spread the drained wood chips in the smoker box and close it; alternatively, spread the wood chips in the foil pan. Place the smoke box or foil pan on a lit burner. *For a charcoal grill*, sprinkle the drained wood chips over the hot coals.

2. Coat the steaks with the oil and season with salt and pepper. When you see the wood chips beginning to smoke, set the steaks on the grill grate and grill them for about 6 minutes per side, or until the meat feels only slightly resilient when pressed with a fingertip, for medium-rare. Transfer the steaks to a carving board and let rest, uncovered, for about 5 minutes.

3. Serve the steaks with the salsa.

Porcini-Braised Beef with Horseradish Mascarpone

Slowly braising meat can turn cheaper cuts into rich, succulent, and hearty dishes. Northern Italy is home of the Slow Cooking movement and they've been cooking meat like this for centuries there, working with earthy ingredients like garlic, onions, and mushrooms. Here I use beef chuck and dried porcini mushrooms. Make enough for leftovers, and you'll have the perfect base for beef sandwiches with arugula and Horseradish Mascarpone.

SERVES: 6

PREP TIME: 20 minutes

COOK TIME: about 4 hours

MAKE-AHEAD: The beef can be braised up to 2 days ahead, cooled, covered, and refrigerated. Rewarm in the pot, covered, over medium-low heat.

1. Preheat the oven to 300°F.

2. Using a clean coffee grinder or spice mill, grind the porcini mushrooms into a powder.

3. Heat a Dutch oven or other wide ovenproof pot over high heat. Season the beef with salt and pepper. Add the oil to the hot pot, then add the beef, and cook, turning the meat occasionally, for about 10 minutes, or until well browned on all sides. Add the wine and stir to scrape up any browned bits on the bottom of the pot, then add the broth, mushrooms, shallots, garlic, thyme, and porcini powder and bring to a simmer.

4. Cover the pot and place it in the oven. Braise the beef, turning the pieces of meat over halfway through the cooking, for 3 hours.

5. Uncover the pot and continue cooking the beef for about 1 hour, or until it is tender enough to pull apart with a spoon and the liquid has reduced by about one-third. Discard the thyme stems.

6. Transfer the beef to four shallow serving bowls, spoon the mushrooms and braising liquid over, and serve with the horseradish mascarpone.

½ ounce dried porcini mushrooms

1 3-pound beef chuck roast, cut into 8 large chunks

Kosher salt and freshly ground black pepper

3 tablespoons olive oil

1 cup dry white wine

3 cups low-sodium beef broth

1 pound white mushrooms, thickly sliced

4 shallots, sliced

8 garlic cloves, chopped

1 bunch fresh thyme

Horseradish Mascarpone (recipe follows)

Horseradish Mascarpone

Horseradish adds a pungent accent to the cream and lovely, rich mascarpone, making it a great accompaniment to steaks or spread for sandwiches. It can be made up to 1 day ahead, covered, and refrigerated. Let stand at room temperature for 30 minutes before serving.

MAKES: about 1½ cups

1 cup mascarpone cheese
⅓ cup finely grated fresh horseradish
¼ cup heavy cream
2 tablespoons fresh lemon juice
Kosher salt and freshly ground black pepper

In a small bowl, mix the mascarpone, horseradish, heavy cream, and lemon juice until blended. Season to taste with salt and pepper.

SERVES: 4

PREP TIME: 25 minutes, plus 30 minutes
for marinating the beef

COOK TIME: 35 minutes

MAKE-AHEAD: The satays can be
marinated for up to 1 day, covered and
refrigerated.

SATAYS

1 bunch cilantro, leaves removed from
stems, stems and leaves reserved

¼ cup soy sauce

1 jalapeño pepper, seeded and chopped

1 1-inch piece fresh ginger, peeled and
finely chopped

2 large garlic cloves, peeled

1 tablespoon light brown sugar

2 teaspoons toasted sesame oil

1 teaspoon freshly ground black pepper

3 tablespoons olive oil

1 pound top sirloin steak, very thinly sliced
against the grain

Bamboo skewers, soaked in water for at least
1 hour

VEGETABLES

1 head bok choy (about 12 ounces),
coarsely chopped into 1½-inch pieces

½ head napa cabbage (about 9 ounces), cut
into 1½-inch pieces

2 ounces snow peas, stringed

½ white onion, thinly sliced

2 tablespoons olive oil

Kosher salt

1½ recipes Jasmine Rice (page 128)
Soy sauce, for drizzling

SPECIAL EQUIPMENT
Grill tray (see Note)

Ginger Beef Satay with Charred Asian Vegetables

Ginger is a natural tenderizer for meat and chicken. That, and a nice
whack from a meat mallet, ensure the steak slices remain tender as they
become crispy on the grill. Chicken thighs are also great in this recipe.

1. To prepare the satays, in a blender or food processor, combine the
   cilantro stems, soy sauce, jalapeño, ginger, garlic, brown sugar, sesame
   oil, and pepper and blend until pureed. With the machine running,
   slowly add 2 tablespoons of the olive oil, blending well.

2. Using the spiked surface of a meat mallet, gently pound both sides of
   the slices of beef to tenderize them. Place the beef slices in a large
   baking dish and coat with the marinade. Cover and marinate for at least
   30 minutes at room temperature, or for up to 1 day in the refrigerator.

3. Prepare a grill for high heat. Place a grill tray on the grill rack.

4. Thread the beef slices lengthwise onto the soaked bamboo skewers so
   that they lie flat. Set aside.

5. To grill the vegetables, in a large bowl, toss the bok choy, cabbage, snow
   peas, and onion with the oil to coat. Season with salt. Transfer the
   vegetables to the hot grill tray and cook, tossing occasionally, for about
   10 minutes, or until they are slightly charred but still crisp-tender.
   Transfer the grill tray to a large baking sheet and set aside.

6. To grill the satays, lightly coat the meat with the remaining
   1 tablespoon oil. Grill for about 2 minutes per side, or until lightly
   charred on the outside but still medium-rare in the center.

7. Divide the rice and vegetables among four plates and drizzle with the soy
   sauce. Top with the satays, sprinkle with the cilantro leaves, and serve.

GRILL TOYS

Just as I have different pots and pans to use on my stove, I've also got fun
tools to cook pretty much anything on my grill. One of my favorite toys is a
grill tray—a sturdy perforated metal sheet that sits on the grill grates and prevents even the smallest ingredient from falling through. With it, I'm able to vir-
tually "stir-fry" veggies that normally would have to be cooked on the
stovetop.

Meat Pies

"Hot pies, cold drinks, get your hot pies, cold drinks here ..." When I think of meat pies, I always think of being at an AFL (Australian Football League) footy game in my hometown of Melbourne, where meat pies, somewhat similar to empanadas, are a signature snack of the game. I'm sharing my recipe for the ultimate homemade version so you can bring a little Aussie footy spirit into your home. A super-buttery pastry dough is filled with seasoned finely chopped or ground meat and minced vegetables. Serve the pies with a simple green salad or—like we Aussies do—with ketchup.

1. To make the filling, heat a large heavy pot over medium-high heat. Add the oil, then add the onion, celery, and carrot and sauté for about 5 minutes, or until the vegetables are tender but not browned. Add the prosciutto and sauté for 2 minutes.

2. Crumble the beef into the pot and season with salt and pepper. Cook, stirring with a wooden spoon to break up the beef, for about 5 minutes, or until the meat is just cooked and no longer pink. Add the chicken livers and cook for about 2 minutes, or until the livers are just cooked and no longer pink. Add the tomato paste and allspice and cook, stirring, for about 2 minutes, or until the tomato paste is well blended.

3. Stir in the wine and cook for about 2 minutes, or until it evaporates completely. Reduce the heat to medium, add the milk, and cook, stirring occasionally, for about 2 minutes, or until the milk has reduced by three-fourths and the sauce is thick and creamy. Sprinkle the flour over the mixture and cook for about 1 minute, stirring constantly, or until well blended.

4. Add the broth, bring to a simmer, and simmer for 25 minutes, or until the liquid has thickened and reduced by one-fourth. Season with salt and pepper. Set the mixture aside to cool. (You should have about 4½ cups filling.)

(continued)

SERVES: 6

PREP TIME: 30 minutes

COOK TIME: 1 hour and 45 minutes

MAKE-AHEAD: The pies can be assembled up to 2 weeks ahead and frozen in an airtight container. Do not thaw before baking, but add 10 minutes to the baking time (50 minutes total).

FILLING

¼ cup extra-virgin olive oil

1 small yellow onion, finely chopped

1 celery stalk, finely chopped

1 small carrot, finely chopped

2 ounces prosciutto di Parma (about 5 slices), finely chopped

1¾ pounds ground beef chuck

Kosher salt and freshly ground black pepper

3 ounces chicken livers (about 3), rinsed, cleaned, and finely chopped

2 tablespoons tomato paste

⅛ teaspoon ground allspice

½ cup dry white wine

½ cup whole milk

2 tablespoons all-purpose flour

3 cups low-sodium beef broth

TO ASSEMBLE THE PIES

All-purpose flour, for dusting

Buttery Pastry Dough (page 147), shaped into 12 disks and chilled

1 large egg

1 tablespoon heavy cream

5. To assemble and bake the pies, position a rack on the lowest rung of the oven and set a baking sheet on the rack. Preheat the oven to 400°F. (Being close to the source of heat will help the bottom crusts bake and brown properly.)

6. On a floured work surface, roll out 1 disk of dough to a 6-inch round about ⅛ inch thick. Line a 5-inch disposable aluminum pie pan with the dough. Repeat with 5 more dough balls and pie pans. Divide the filling among the pans, using about ¾ cup filling per pie.

7. Roll out the remaining 6 dough pieces to 6-inch rounds and lay them over the filling. Trim the dough overhang to ½ inch. Pinch the bottom and top crusts together to seal, and fold them under. Crimp the edges. Using your finger, make a hole in the center of each top crust.

8. In a small bowl, whisk the egg and cream to blend. Using a pastry brush, lightly brush the tops of the pies with the egg-cream mixture.

9. Place the pies on the preheated baking sheet in the oven and bake for about 40 minutes, or until the crust is deep golden and the filling is bubbling. If the crust begins to brown before the filling bubbles, tent the pies with foil. Let the pies cool on a wire rack until warm before serving.

Teriyaki Beef Ribs with Enoki Mushrooms

Korean-style or flanken-style beef short ribs are a lesser-known cut of meat but they're well worth getting acquainted with. They're basically thinly sliced short ribs that become super tender and tasty when marinated for a few hours and cooked for just a minute or two per side. Pick up this cut from your local butcher or Asian grocer. The ribs can also be grilled on the barbecue, along with a bunch of whole scallions, and served with Jasmine Rice (page 128). If you can't find enoki mushrooms, thinly sliced stemmed shiitake mushrooms are fine too.

SERVES: 4

PREP TIME: 10 minutes, plus at least 3 hours for marinating the meat

COOK TIME: 25 minutes

MAKE-AHEAD: The teriyaki sauce can be made up to 1 week ahead, covered, and refrigerated.

½ cup mirin (sweet Japanese rice wine)

½ cup soy sauce

¼ cup packed light brown sugar

¼ cup sake

8 ⅓-inch-thick Korean-style beef short ribs (flanken-style; about 4 ounces each)

1 tablespoon finely chopped peeled fresh ginger

¼ cup canola oil

4 ounces shishito or Padrón peppers (about 20)

¼ cup low-sodium beef broth

2 ounces enoki mushrooms, stems trimmed

1. To make the teriyaki sauce, in a small bowl, stir the mirin, soy sauce, brown sugar, and sake to dissolve the sugar.

2. In a resealable plastic bag, combine the ribs, ¼ cup of the teriyaki sauce, the ginger, and 1 tablespoon of the oil. Seal the bag and marinate in the refrigerator for at least 3 hours, or for as long as overnight.

3. Heat a large heavy skillet over medium-high heat. Add 1 tablespoon of the oil and the shishito peppers and cook, turning occasionally, for about 4 minutes, or until the peppers are softened and charred. Transfer the peppers to a plate and set aside in a warm spot.

4. Meanwhile, heat a very large heavy skillet over high heat. Remove the ribs from the bag, discard the marinade, and pat the ribs dry. Add 1 tablespoon of the oil to the hot skillet. When the oil is very hot, add 4 of the ribs and cook for about 1½ minutes per side, or until heavily caramelized and cooked through. Transfer the ribs to a plate. Pour off the fat from the pan and wipe out the pan. Repeat with the remaining 1 tablespoon oil and the remaining 4 ribs. Set the ribs aside to rest for 5 minutes.

5. Wipe out the pan you used for the ribs and add the broth and remaining teriyaki sauce to the pan. Simmer for about 2 minutes, or until the sauce thickens slightly. Add the mushrooms and simmer for about 2 minutes, or until the sauce is reduced by half and glossy and the mushrooms are tender. Remove the pan from the heat, return all the ribs and any accumulated juices to the pan, and toss with the sauce to coat.

6. Place the ribs on four plates, with the teriyaki-mushroom sauce, and garnish with the blistered shishito peppers.

Grilled Lamb Chops with Kalamata Salsa Verde

SERVES: 4

PREP TIME: 15 minutes

COOK TIME: 10 minutes

MAKE-AHEAD: The salsa verde must be made at least 4 hours ahead and can be made up to 1 day ahead, covered, and refrigerated.

KALAMATA SALSA VERDE

2 lemons

⅓ cup finely chopped scallions (white and green parts)

⅓ cup pitted kalamata olives, coarsely chopped

¼ cup finely chopped drained capers

¼ cup finely chopped fresh flat-leaf parsley

¼ cup extra-virgin olive oil

2 tablespoons finely chopped shallots

1 tablespoon finely chopped fresh oregano

1 teaspoon finely chopped fresh rosemary

Kosher salt and freshly ground black pepper

LAMB

8 lamb chops (about 1¾ pounds total)

Kosher salt and freshly ground black pepper

1 tablespoon extra-virgin olive oil

Shallot-Mint Yogurt Sauce (recipe follows)

Grilled Flatbreads with Garlic-Rosemary Oil (page 230)

We Aussies love our lamb, and a leg roast was a staple meal during my childhood. A quicker alternative are tender and succulent chops that only need a few minutes on the grill. This Greek-inspired recipe pairs fragrant minty yogurt with the smokiness of grilled lamb, and the olive salsa drives that Mediterranean flavor home. The yogurt and salsa verde go nicely with any cut of lamb.

1. To make the salsa verde, finely grate the zest of 1 lemon (about 1 tablespoon) into a small bowl. Mix in the scallions, olives, capers, parsley, oil, shallots, oregano, and rosemary. Squeeze ¼ cup of juice from the lemons and stir the juice into the salsa. Season to taste with salt and pepper. Cover and refrigerate for at least 4 hours.

2. To grill the lamb chops, prepare a grill for medium-high heat.

3. Season the lamb chops with salt and pepper and rub them with the oil. Grill the chops for about 4 minutes, or until well browned on the bottom. Turn the chops over and grill for about 3 minutes longer for medium-rare. Transfer the chops to four plates and let rest for 5 minutes.

4. Spoon the salsa verde over the lamb chops and serve the yogurt sauce and flatbreads alongside.

Shallot-Mint Yogurt Sauce

Lemon and mint are naturally fresh and fragrant ingredients; add them to Greek yogurt and you've got a bright sauce for lamb and chicken dishes. Or serve as a dip for grilled flatbreads (see page 230) or pita chips. The sauce can be made up to 1 day ahead, covered, and refrigerated.

MAKES: 2½ cups

2 cups plain 2%-fat Greek yogurt
½ cup loosely packed fresh mint leaves, finely chopped
¼ cup finely chopped shallots (about 2)
2 teaspoons finely grated lemon zest
Kosher salt and freshly ground black pepper

In a medium bowl, mix the yogurt, mint, shallots, and lemon zest. Season to taste with salt and pepper. Cover and refrigerate for at least 30 minutes before serving.

Herb-Crusted Rack of Lamb with Fennel

Have you ever tasted Italian porchetta? Most often, you see it as a pork roast where pork belly is wrapped around a pork loin and seasoned assertively with fennel, rosemary, and garlic. It is truly good food. It's also a beast of a meal. So I decided to take the flavors of a traditional porchetta and transfer them to a decidedly leaner cut of lamb. The result is a meal that is heavy on delicious flavors and light on time.

SERVES: 4

PREP TIME: 15 minutes

COOK TIME: 25 minutes

MAKE-AHEAD: The herbs can be chopped up to 4 hours ahead, covered, and refrigerated.

2 large fennel bulbs with fronds
½ cup olive oil
Kosher salt and freshly ground black pepper
2 small racks of lamb (1 pound each)
2 garlic cloves, chopped
¼ cup chopped fresh flat-leaf parsley
½ teaspoon chopped fresh rosemary
½ teaspoon fennel seeds, crushed
2 tablespoons Dijon mustard

1. Preheat the oven to 425°F.

2. Trim the stalks from the fennel bulbs and finely chop enough of the fronds to equal about ¼ cup; set aside in a small bowl. Thinly slice the fennel bulbs from the stalk end through the base. On a heavy baking sheet, toss the sliced fennel with 1 tablespoon of the oil, seasoning with salt and pepper. Spread the fennel over the baking sheet and set aside.

3. Season the lamb with salt and pepper. Heat a large skillet over medium-high heat. Add 2 tablespoons of the oil, then add the lamb and cook, turning occasionally, for about 6 minutes, or until the racks are golden brown all over. Set the lamb fat side up atop the fennel on the baking sheet.

4. Mix the garlic, parsley, rosemary, fennel seeds, mustard, and the remaining 5 tablespoons oil into the chopped fennel fronds; season with salt and pepper. Spread the mixture all over the lamb.

5. Roast the lamb for about 18 minutes, or until an instant-read thermometer inserted into the thickest part of the meat registers 130°F for medium-rare. Transfer to a cutting board and let rest for 5 minutes.

6. Cut the lamb into double chops and serve with the roasted fennel.

Stracci with Braised Lamb Ragù

SERVES: 4

PREP TIME: 10 minutes

COOK TIME: 1 hour and 20 minutes

MAKE-AHEAD: The ragù can be made up to 3 days ahead, cooled, covered, and refrigerated. Rewarm the ragù in a pot, covered, over medium-low heat, adding some water, as needed, to reach the desired consistency.

RAGÙ

2 large bone-in lamb shanks (about 2 pounds total)

Kosher salt and freshly ground black pepper

4 teaspoons olive oil

½ onion, sliced

3 garlic cloves, smashed

1 Fresno chile, finely chopped

2 cups canned crushed tomatoes

1 cup water

15 Castelvetrano or other brined green olives, pitted and quartered

CHILE GREMOLATA

2 tablespoons chopped fresh flat-leaf parsley

Grated zest of 1 lemon

1 Fresno chile, finely chopped

10 ounces lasagne sheets, broken into 2-inch pieces

1 tablespoon unsalted butter

2 tablespoons freshly grated Parmesan cheese, plus more for serving

There are three things that elevate this family-style pasta dish from good to incredible: the silky, falling-off-the-bone tomato-braised lamb cooked in a pressure cooker; the rustic stracci pasta (*stracci* means "rags" in Italian, and it refers to the shape of the pasta—here I just use lasagne sheets that have been broken into pieces); and the zesty gremolata. Gremolata is an Italian chopped herb condiment and this version is sparked with a chile bite. A very satisfying dish served as is or paired with a side of seasonal veggies, a green salad, and a plummy dry red wine. I always make extra ragù to enjoy during the week.

1. To make the lamb ragù, season the lamb shanks with salt and pepper. Heat a large pressure cooker over high heat. Add 2 teaspoons of the oil and then the lamb and cook, turning occasionally for about 8 minutes, or until browned on all sides. Remove the lamb from the pot and discard the fat.

2. Reduce the heat to medium. Add the remaining 2 teaspoons oil, the sliced onion, garlic, and chile to the pot and cook, stirring often, for about 8 minutes, or until the onion is tender and beginning to caramelize. Add 1½ cups of the crushed tomatoes and the water and return the lamb to the pot.

3. Lock the pressure cooker lid in place and bring to high pressure over high heat, about 15 minutes. Reduce the heat to low to stabilize the pressure and cook the lamb for 50 minutes. Remove from the heat and allow the pressure to subside on its own, about 20 minutes.

4. Unlock the pressure cooker and remove the lid, tilting it away from you to allow the steam to escape. Spoon any scum and oil from the top of the braising liquid. Set aside until the lamb is cool enough to handle, then pull the meat from the bones; discard the bones and cartilage and set the meat aside.

5. Add the remaining ½ cup crushed tomatoes to the pressure cooker, bring to a boil over medium-high heat, and boil for about 5 minutes, or until the sauce is reduced by one-third. Add the lamb meat to the sauce

(continued)

and stir in the olives. Remove the pot from the heat and season the ragù to taste with salt and pepper. Cover to keep hot while the pasta cooks.

6. Meanwhile, to make the gremolata, in a small bowl, mix the parsley, lemon zest, and chopped chile. Set aside.

7. To cook the pasta, bring a large pot of salted water to a boil over high heat. Add the pasta and cook, stirring occasionally, for about 8 minutes, or until tender but firm to the bite. Drain the pasta, reserving about ½ cup of the cooking water.

8. Return the ragù to a gentle simmer over medium-low heat. Gently stir the pasta into the ragù and cook for about 1 minute, adding the reserved pasta water to moisten the mixture as needed. Remove the pot from the heat and stir in the butter and Parmesan cheese.

9. Divide the pasta among four bowls. Sprinkle the gremolata and a little more Parmesan cheese over the top and serve immediately.

VARIATION If you don't have a pressure cooker, use a heavy medium casserole pot instead for steps 1 and 2. For step 3, cover the casserole pot and place it in a 300°F oven. Cook for about 2½ hours, turning the lamb over halfway through cooking and spooning off any scum and oil from the top of the braising liquid. Set aside until the lamb is cool enough to handle, then pull the meat from the bone, and discard the bones and cartilage. Continue as directed in steps 5 through 9.

Roasted Salmon and Beets with Herb Vinaigrette

SERVES: 4

PREP TIME: 20 minutes

COOK TIME: 35 minutes

4 medium beets, preferably golden (1 pound total), scrubbed and very thinly sliced lengthwise (see Note)

6 tablespoons extra-virgin olive oil

Kosher salt and freshly ground black pepper

1 1½-pound skinless salmon fillet (from the head end)

1 tablespoon finely chopped fresh chives

I tablespoon finely chopped fresh flat-leaf parsley

1 tablespoon finely chopped fresh tarragon

3 tablespoons finely chopped shallots

1 tablespoon grated lemon zest

¼ cup fresh lemon juice

4 cups mixed baby greens

When you look at the cooking time for this recipe, you may be surprised to find that it is only 35 minutes. Because the beets are sliced into thin rounds, they'll cook much faster, and high heat quickly roasts both the beets and the salmon. For easy cleanup, everything is cooked on the same baking sheet (you can also use a large baking dish to serve it family-style). Accompany the salmon with Crispy Potato Cakes (page 134) or Buttered Buns (page 139), if desired.

1. Preheat the oven to 450°F.

2. On a baking sheet, toss the beets with 1½ tablespoons of the oil to coat. Season with salt and pepper. Arrange the beets in the center of the baking sheet, forming a bed large enough to hold the salmon. Roast the beets for about 20 minutes, or until crisp-tender.

3. Place the salmon on top of the beets. Brush the salmon with ½ tablespoon of the oil and season with salt and pepper. In a large bowl, mix the chives, parsley, and tarragon. Sprinkle all but 1 tablespoon of the mixed herbs over the salmon.

4. Roast the salmon for about 15 minutes, or until cooked to medium-rare doneness so it is slightly rosy in the center. Remove from the oven.

5. Meanwhile, whisk the remaining 4 tablespoons oil, the shallots, lemon zest, and juice into the remaining mixed herbs. Season the dressing to taste with salt and pepper.

6. Toss the mixed greens with 2 tablespoons of the dressing. Drizzle the remaining dressing over and around the salmon and beets and serve the greens alongside.

THE LOWDOWN ON BEETS

You can use any kind of beets you like in this beautiful dinner, but I particularly love the way golden beets look against the salmon. Or, if you see them at the market, use Chioggia beets, also known as candy-cane beets and named for their red-and-white peppermint-candy-like pattern (don't worry, they don't taste like mint). And hey, if only red beets are available, use them.

Maple-Glazed Planked Salmon

Brining the salmon in the maple-saltwater gives it a sweet-salty flavor and moist texture. Cooking the fish on the cedar plank imparts a woodsy, smoky flavor and eliminates any worry of the fish sticking to the grill. Cedar planks are inexpensive and can be found at your local barbecue store or online. This dish matches with many sides and salads, including Green Bean and Cherry Tomato Gratin (page 133), Quick-Braised Spring Vegetables (page 127), Cheddar-and-Corn Cream Biscuits (page 136), and My Favorite Potato Salad (page 123).

SERVES: 4

PREP TIME: 20 minutes, plus at least 1 hour for brining the salmon

COOK TIME: 20 minutes

MAKE-AHEAD: The salmon can be brined for up to 1 day.

3 cups warm water

¾ cup packed light brown sugar

⅓ cup pure maple syrup

¼ cup kosher salt

1 1½-pound skinless salmon fillet (from the head end)

Olive oil, for brushing

SPECIAL EQUIPMENT

1 14 x 5-inch untreated cedar plank, soaked in water for 2 hours

1. In a 13 x 9-inch glass or ceramic baking dish, stir the water, brown sugar, syrup, and salt until the sugar and salt dissolve. Set aside until completely cool.

2. Place the salmon fillet in the brine. The brine should completely cover the salmon. Cover and refrigerate for at least 1 hour.

3. Prepare a grill for cooking over indirect heat: *For a gas grill,* heat one burner on high heat; leave the other burner(s) turned off. *For a charcoal grill,* place all of the lit briquettes in one side of the grill, leaving the other side empty.

4. Remove the salmon from the brine and transfer it to a rack set over a small baking sheet. Pat dry.

5. Remove the cedar plank from the soaking water and pat dry. Place the plank on the grill grate over the fire for 2 minutes, or until the plank is heated through. Flip the plank over and move to the other (cool) side of the grill grate. Brush the plank lightly with olive oil and place the salmon on the plank.

6. Close the grill lid and cook the salmon for about 15 minutes, rotating the plank 180 degrees midway through cooking, or until the salmon feels flaky on the outside but has a rosy center. Using oven mitts, remove the plank from the grill and set it on a baking sheet. Let stand for 3 minutes.

7. Using a metal fish spatula, transfer the salmon to a platter, or cut into 4 pieces and transfer to plates. Alternatively, serve the salmon from the plank.

Grilled Tuna with Rémoulade Sauce

SERVES: 8

PREP TIME: 15 minutes

COOK TIME: 6 minutes

MAKE-AHEAD: The rémoulade sauce can be made up to 3 days ahead, covered, and refrigerated. Any remaining grilled tuna can be covered and refrigerated up to 1 day to enjoy as leftovers.

RÉMOULADE

½ cup Aïoli (page 30) or mayonnaise

½ cup crème fraîche

⅔ cup finely chopped scallions (white and green parts)

¼ cup drained capers

1 tablespoon finely chopped fresh tarragon

Finely grated zest of 2 lemons

3 tablespoons fresh lemon juice

2 garlic cloves, finely chopped

TUNA

8 5-ounce albacore tuna steaks

2 tablespoons olive oil

Kosher salt and freshly ground black pepper

SPECIAL EQUIPMENT

2 cups mesquite or apple wood chips, soaked in cold water for 1 hour

Smoker wood chip box or a 13 x 9-inch aluminum foil pan (if using a gas grill)

This recipe may seem simple, but it is, in fact, genius! I like to grill 8 fish steaks even when I'm just making dinner for 4, so I can combine the leftover fish and rémoulade sauce the next day to make tuna salad sandwiches or tuna melts. For tuna salad, mix equal parts leftover grilled tuna and rémoulade sauce. Serve with a mixed green salad and grilled bread for a quick, stress-free dinner.

1. To make the rémoulade, in a medium bowl, whisk the aïoli, crème fraîche, scallions, capers, tarragon, lemon zest, lemon juice, and garlic together. Cover and refrigerate while preparing the tuna.

2. To cook the tuna, prepare a grill for high heat: *For a gas grill*, spread the drained wood chips in the smoker box and close it; alternatively, spread the wood chips in the foil pan. Place the smoke box or foil pan on a lit burner. *For a charcoal grill*, sprinkle the drained wood chips over the hot coals.

3. Coat the tuna with the oil and season with salt and pepper. When you see the wood chips beginning to smoke, set the tuna on the grill grate over the wood chips, close the lid, and grill the tuna for about 3 minutes per side, or until it feels flaky on the outside but is still medium-rare when pierced in the thickest part with the tip of a small knife. Using a metal fish spatula, transfer the tuna to plates or a platter and let stand for at least 3 minutes.

4. Serve the tuna hot or cold with the rémoulade sauce.

Whole Grilled Branzino with Soy-Ginger Sauce

Cooking fish on the grill imparts a delicious smoky flavor to the fish. This fantastic whole round branzino needs to turn over once and the skin prevents the flesh from falling apart and sticking to the grill. Serve these beauties on a platter in the center of the table with this simple sesame-soy sauce and grill some green beans to go alongside.

1. Prepare a grill for medium-high heat.

2. Using a large sharp knife, cut 3 diagonal slits into both sides of each fish (this will allow the flavors of the marinade to penetrate the flesh). Divide the sliced ginger, scallion pieces, halved garlic, and chopped cilantro between the cavities of the fish. Put the fish on a platter or tray.

3. In a medium bowl, mix the chopped ginger, two-thirds of the sliced scallions, the chopped garlic, olive oil, soy sauce, sugar, and sesame oil. Season with pepper. Spoon ½ tablespoon of the marinade over both sides of each fish and marinate the fish for 5 minutes. Reserve the remaining marinade to serve as the sauce.

4. Oil the grill grates. Place the fish on the grill, close the lid, and cook for about 4 minutes per side, or until the flesh is firm, white, and flaky but still moist and juicy and the skin is crisp. Transfer the fish to two platters.

5. Garnish with the remaining sliced scallions and the cilantro leaves. Serve with the rice and the reserved sauce, allowing everyone at the table to serve themselves from the platters.

SERVES: 4

PREP TIME: 15 minutes, plus 5 minutes for marinating the fish

COOK TIME: 8 minutes

MAKE-AHEAD: The marinade can be made up to 1 day ahead, covered, and refrigerated.

2 1- to 1¼-pound whole branzini, scaled, gutted, and fins removed (ask your fishmonger to do this)

3 thumb-size pieces fresh ginger, peeled, 1 thinly sliced, 2 finely chopped

4 scallions, trimmed, 1 cut crosswise into ½-inch pieces, 3 thinly sliced

3 garlic cloves, 1 crushed and halved, 2 finely chopped

1 tablespoon chopped fresh cilantro, plus whole leaves for garnish

⅓ cup olive oil

⅓ cup soy sauce

1 tablespoon sugar

1½ teaspoons toasted sesame oil

Freshly ground black pepper

Jasmine Rice (page 128)

HANDY HINTS

It's easy to flip a whole fish on the grill, but if you're a little leery about it, you can use a fish grill basket; it eliminates all the worry. Just lightly oil the grill basket, place the fish in the basket, and close it. Oil the grill grates, place the basket on the grates, and cook the fish as directed.

To fillet the cooked branzino, make a cut behind the head, cutting through to the backbone. Make a second incision just before the tail. Run the tip of a sharp knife along the backbone and down to the spine, gently removing the top fillet off the spine. Holding the tail, lift the spine and head off the bottom fillet.

Grilled Crab Legs with Avocado Chimichurri

SERVES: 4

PREP TIME: 20 minutes

COOK TIME: about 4 minutes

8 large king crab legs (about 4 pounds)

¼ cup fresh lemon juice

¼ cup red wine vinegar

2 garlic cloves, finely chopped

1½ teaspoons kosher salt

1 teaspoon red pepper flakes

1 teaspoon dried oregano

½ teaspoon freshly ground black pepper

½ cup olive oil

½ cup chopped fresh cilantro

½ cup chopped fresh flat-leaf parsley

2 firm but ripe avocados, halved, pitted, peeled, and cubed

4½-inch-thick slices ciabatta bread or other rustic bread

Do not turn the page! Crab legs sound fancy, but this is a super-simple recipe for a special dinner. Just get your hands on the crab legs, filled with sweet, white meat (what a delicacy!), and in just a few simple steps, you're there. Crab legs are typically sold cooked and frozen and can be found at your local fishmonger, farmers' markets, and in the seafood department of some supermarkets. I like to serve them up on a platter and encourage my family and friends to pull the meat out of the shell themselves. If crab is not for you, grilled jumbo shrimp taste great with the chimichurri too.

1. Using kitchen shears, cut a long lengthwise slit down the bottom of each crab shell.

2. In a small bowl, stir the lemon juice, vinegar, garlic, salt, red pepper flakes, oregano, and black pepper together. Whisk in the oil to blend, then stir in the cilantro and parsley. Gently fold in the avocados.

3. Prepare a grill for medium-high heat.

4. Grill the crab legs cut side up for about 4 minutes, or until heated through. At the same time, grill the bread for about 2 minutes per side, or until warm, golden, and crisp on the outside.

5. Spoon the avocado mixture atop the toasts and serve immediately with the crab legs, using crab crackers to split open the legs and remove the tender meat.

CHIMICHURRI

Chimichurri is a favorite Argentinean sauce made of chopped parsley, cilantro, garlic, vinegar, and oil. For this version, cubes of avocado are folded into the sauce. It's addictive spooned atop smoky grilled bread.

Risotto with Shrimp, Arugula, and Lemon Cream

This super simple risotto is elevated by a dollop of lemon cream. If you'd like a veggie risotto instead, switch out the shrimp for a handful of spring peas and a bunch of chopped asparagus and replace the chicken broth with vegetable broth.

SERVES: 4

PREP TIME: 10 minutes

COOK TIME: 25 minutes

1. In a small heavy saucepan, bring the chicken stock and water to a simmer over high heat. Turn off the heat and cover to keep warm.

2. Meanwhile, heat a large deep heavy nonstick skillet over medium heat. Add the oil, then add the garlic and cook for about 1 minute, or until golden brown. Add the onion and cook for about 2 minutes, or until softened. Add the rice and stir for about 1 minute, or until it is well coated. Add the wine and stir for about 1 minute, or until most of the wine has evaporated.

3. Add 1 cup of the hot stock mixture to the rice and cook, stirring almost constantly and keeping the mixture at a steady simmer, until it is absorbed. Continue to add the hot stock mixture 1 cup at a time, stirring until each addition is almost completely absorbed before adding more, and cook for a total of about 18 minutes, or until the rice is creamy but still al dente (you may not need all of the stock).

4. Add the shrimp and cook, stirring, for about 3 minutes, or until the shrimp is just opaque throughout. Remove the pan from the heat and stir in the butter, parsley, and Parmesan cheese. Stir in the arugula and lemon juice and season to taste with salt.

5. In a medium bowl, whisk the heavy cream with the lemon zest just until thickened. Divide the risotto among four wide serving bowls. Garnish each one with a dollop of the whipped cream and some pepper and serve immediately.

3 cups low-sodium chicken broth

3 cups water

2 tablespoons olive oil

3 garlic cloves, finely chopped

½ medium onion, finely chopped (about ½ cup)

1¾ cups Arborio rice

½ cup dry white wine

1 pound peeled and deveined large shrimp (16 to 20 per pound), cut into ½-inch pieces

2 tablespoons (¼ stick) unsalted butter

1 tablespoon finely chopped fresh flat-leaf parsley

¼ cup freshly grated Parmesan cheese

2 cups loosely packed arugula (preferably wild or baby)

2 tablespoons fresh lemon juice

Kosher salt

½ cup heavy cream

1 tablespoon grated lemon zest

Freshly ground black pepper

THE ABSORPTION METHOD

Risotto rice is cooked by the absorption method rather than by boiling or steaming. Stock is added gradually to the rice, slowly plumping up the grains. Simmering the risotto, not boiling, is essential to ensure a creamy yet al dente consistency.

Almond Falafel

SERVES: 6

PREP TIME: 15 minutes

COOK TIME: 8 minutes

MAKE-AHEAD: The falafel mixture (without the baking powder) can be prepared up to 12 hours ahead, covered, and refrigerated.

½ onion, coarsely chopped (½ cup)

4 garlic cloves

1 tablespoon ground coriander

1½ teaspoons ground cumin

1½ teaspoons kosher salt, plus more to taste

½ teaspoon cayenne pepper

⅔ cup packed fresh flat-leaf parsley leaves (from about 1 bunch)

½ cup packed fresh cilantro leaves (from about 1 bunch)

1 cup raw whole almonds

2 cups drained canned chickpeas, rinsed

⅓ cup all-purpose flour

2 tablespoons toasted sesame seeds

1½ teaspoons baking powder

Canola oil, for deep-frying

ACCOMPANIMENTS

6 Grilled Flatbreads (page 230) or pita breads, warmed

Tahini Sauce (recipe follows)

½ head romaine lettuce, very thinly sliced (about 1½ cups)

¼ head green cabbage, very thinly sliced (about 1½ cups)

½ red onion, very thinly sliced (¾ cup)

1 tomato, sliced

1 Persian cucumber or ½ English (hothouse) cucumber, thinly sliced

Traditionally, falafel is made with uncooked chickpeas that have been soaked overnight just until partially softened, resulting in a crunchy texture. But with that method, falafel can't very well be made on a whim. Using canned chickpeas instead lets you skip the wait, and here the almonds mimic the texture of semisoftened chickpeas, making this satisfying through and through.

1. In a food processor, combine the onion, garlic, coriander, cumin, salt, and cayenne and pulse until the onion is finely chopped. Add the parsley and cilantro and pulse until the herbs are coarsely chopped. Add the almonds and pulse until they are coarsely chopped. Add the chickpeas and pulse until roughly chopped; do not overblend so that some chunky pieces of almonds and chickpeas still remain.

2. Transfer the mixture to a bowl and stir in the flour and sesame seeds. If you're going to fry the falafel right away, mix in the baking powder. If you're going to fry the falafel later, cover the mixture and refrigerate for up to 12 hours; stir in the baking powder just before you shape and fry the falafel.

3. In a large heavy pot, heat 3 inches of oil to 350°F. Preheat the oven to 200°F. Line a large baking sheet with 3 layers of paper towels.

4. Using about 1½ tablespoons of the chickpea mixture for each one, form the mixture into balls that are about the size of small walnuts. Working in batches, fry the falafel for 3 to 4 minutes, or until golden brown. Transfer the fried falafel to the paper towels to drain and season with salt. Place the falafel in a baking dish and keep warm in the oven while you fry the remaining falafel balls.

5. Arrange the hot falafel and the flatbreads on a platter and place the tahini sauce in a bowl. Serve with the remaining accompaniments.

Tahini Sauce

For this recipe, I add garlic, fresh lemon juice, parsley, and cilantro to thick tahini paste to transform it into a flavorful sauce. Serve with kebabs or grilled chicken, lamb, or beef, as well as the falafel, or spread it on sandwiches and wraps. The tahini sauce can be made up to 1 day ahead, covered and refrigerated.

MAKES: 1⅓ cups

1 garlic clove
½ cup tahini paste
¼ cup packed fresh cilantro leaves
¼ cup packed fresh flat-leaf parsley leaves
¼ cup fresh lemon juice
About ½ cup cold water
Kosher salt and freshly ground black pepper

In a food processor, finely chop the garlic. Blend in the tahini, cilantro, and parsley. With the machine running, add the lemon juice. Scrape down the sides and bottom of the bowl. Slowly blend in enough cold water to form a sauce with the consistency of heavy cream. Season to taste with salt and pepper.

Winter Vegetable Curry with Chile-Mint Chutney

SERVES: 4

PREP TIME: 15 minutes

COOK TIME: 35 minutes

MAKE-AHEAD: The curry can be made up to 2 days ahead, covered, and refrigerated. Rewarm, covered, over low heat.

1 tablespoon grapeseed oil

1 small onion, cut into small dice (1 cup)

1 garlic clove, finely chopped

1 tablespoon finely chopped peeled fresh ginger

1 small jalapeño pepper, finely chopped

1 teaspoon ground coriander

1 teaspoon ground turmeric

½ teaspoon ground cardamom

½ teaspoon ground cumin

3 parsnips, peeled, halved lengthwise, tough core removed, and cut into ¾-inch pieces (about 2 cups)

2 rutabagas, peeled and cut into ¾-inch pieces (about 2 cups)

½ small kabocha squash, peeled and cut into ¾-inch pieces (about 3 cups)

½ head cauliflower, cut into large florets (about 3 cups)

1 13½-ounce can unsweetened coconut milk

¼ cup water

Kosher salt

Chile-Mint Chutney (recipe follows)

Your meat-free Mondays will become all the more interesting with this vibrant vegan curry. You'll love the tender, flavorful veggies and fresh, zingy chutney. Be sure to serve fluffy Jasmine Rice (page 128), warm naan bread, or Grilled Flatbreads with Garlic-Rosemary Oil (page 230) to soak up the sauce.

1. Heat a large heavy pot over medium heat. Add the oil, then add the onion and sauté for about 8 minutes, or until tender. Add the garlic, ginger, jalapeño, coriander, turmeric, cardamom, and cumin and cook for about 2 minutes, stirring frequently, or until aromatic. Add the parsnips, rutabagas, and squash and sauté for about 2 minutes to coat with the aromatics and spices.

2. Add the cauliflower, coconut milk, and water and bring to a simmer. Cover and simmer gently until the vegetables are tender, about 20 minutes. Season with salt.

3. Spoon the curry into bowls. Spoon the chutney on top and serve.

Chile-Mint Chutney

This chutney gives Indian curries, meaty sandwiches, and even steamed potatoes a nice flavor kick. It can be made up to 6 hours ahead, covered, and refrigerated.

MAKES: 1 cup

1 cup tightly packed fresh cilantro leaves

1 cup tightly packed fresh mint leaves

¼ cup fresh lemon juice

¼ cup dry-roasted peanuts

2 serrano chiles, seeded and thinly sliced

1 tablespoon finely chopped peeled fresh ginger

2½ tablespoons water

½ teaspoon kosher salt, or to taste

In a small food processor, combine the cilantro, mint, lemon juice, peanuts, chiles, ginger, and water and process until smooth. Season with the salt.

Potato and Zucchini Enchiladas with Habanero Salsa

Enchiladas work as both party food and comfort food. Here the warm tortillas are stuffed with a hearty spiced 'n' diced potato and zucchini filling and then topped with a smoky salsa that packs just enough heat to send you back for a second helping. The potato-zucchini mixture can also be served on its own as a side for grilled steak and sausages, stirred into pasta, or mixed into a frittata. Habanero chiles are very spicy—use at your discretion.

SERVES: 4

PREP TIME: 25 minutes

COOK TIME: 45 minutes

MAKE-AHEAD: The salsa and the vegetable filling can be made up to 1 day ahead, covered separately and refrigerated. Rewarm the salsa over medium-low heat before serving.

3 ripe tomatoes (1¼ pounds total), cored

3 fresh Anaheim chiles (8 ounces total)

½ to 1 habanero chile, seeded

7 tablespoons olive oil

Kosher salt and freshly ground black pepper

10 fresh cilantro sprigs

3 garlic cloves, 1 whole (but peeled), 2 finely chopped

2 russet (baking) potatoes (about 1 pound total), cut into ½-inch dice

1 zucchini, cut into ½-inch dice (1½ cups)

½ white onion, finely diced (1 cup)

8 corn tortillas

1 cup coarsely crumbled Cotija or feta cheese

1 large or 2 small scallions, trimmed and thinly sliced

⅓ cup sour cream

1. To make the salsa and filling, preheat the broiler.

2. Line a baking sheet with foil and put the tomatoes and chiles on it. Rub 1 tablespoon of the oil over the tomatoes and chiles and sprinkle with salt and pepper. Broil, turning as needed, until the tomatoes and chiles are tender and their skins have charred, about 10 minutes for the habanero, 15 minutes for the Anaheim chiles, and 20 minutes for the tomatoes. When the Anaheim chiles are done, transfer them to a bowl, cover with plastic wrap, and set aside until cool enough to handle. When the habanero and tomatoes are done, transfer to a plate and let cool slightly. Peel, seed, and coarsely chop the Anaheim chiles; set aside.

3. Meanwhile, remove the leaves from the cilantro and place the stems in a blender. Coarsely chop the leaves and reserve in a medium bowl. Add the whole garlic clove, the broiled tomatoes, habanero, and any accumulated juices to the blender and blend until smooth. Season the salsa to taste with salt. Set aside.

4. Heat a large heavy nonstick skillet over medium heat. Add 2 tablespoons of the oil, then add the potatoes and cook for about 5 minutes, or until they are beginning to soften. Add the zucchini, onion, and the chopped garlic and sauté for about 5 minutes, or until the potatoes are tender. Stir in the chopped Anaheim chiles and ¼ cup of the salsa and season to taste with salt. Set aside to cool.

5. To assemble the enchiladas, preheat the oven to 450°F. Line a small baking sheet with paper towels.

(continued)

6. In a small skillet, heat the remaining 4 tablespoons olive oil over medium heat. Add 1 tortilla to the pan and cook for about 20 seconds per side, or until just pliable. Using tongs, transfer the tortilla to the paper-towel-lined baking sheet to absorb any excess oil. Repeat with the remaining tortillas, layering them between paper towels.

7. Spoon about ⅓ cup of the potato mixture over the bottom third of one tortilla, then roll up, and place seam side down in a 13 x 9-inch baking dish. Repeat with the remaining tortillas and filling.

8. Bake the enchiladas, uncovered, for about 10 minutes, or just until heated through. Reheat the remaining salsa.

9. Drizzle about ⅔ cup of the remaining salsa over the enchiladas, then sprinkle the cheese, scallions, and reserved cilantro leaves over the top. Serve with the sour cream and pass the remaining salsa at the table to spoon onto plates when serving.

Spaghettini with Lemon and Ricotta

SERVES: 4

PREP TIME: 5 minutes

COOK TIME: 6 minutes

12 ounces spaghettini

¾ cup Homemade Ricotta (recipe follows) or good-quality fresh whole-milk ricotta

1½ tablespoons extra-virgin olive oil

½ teaspoon freshly ground black pepper

2 lemons

Kosher salt

This lovely, light pasta dish shows off a perfect balance of just a few simple ingredients: mild, creamy Homemade Ricotta and zesty, bold lemons. Spaghettini is best when slightly al dente; its delicate bite and texture are lost if it's overcooked. You could add sautéed or roasted veggies, but most often, I like to serve this just as is.

1. Bring a large pot of salted water to a boil over high heat. Add the spaghettini and cook, stirring occasionally, for about 6 minutes, or until it is tender but still firm to the bite. Drain the spaghettini, reserving about ½ cup of the cooking water.

2. Meanwhile, in a large bowl, mix the ricotta, oil, and pepper. Grate the zest of 1 lemon over the ricotta and mix it in. Season with salt.

3. Add the spaghettini to the ricotta mixture and stir well to coat, adding the reserved cooking water to moisten as needed. Season to taste with salt.

4. Divide the pasta among 4 plates. Finely grate the zest of the remaining lemon over the pasta and serve immediately.

Homemade Ricotta

There's something so rewarding about making your own cheese, and homemade ricotta is the easiest one to make. Usually it's made with just milk and lemon, but I like to mix in cream and buttermilk for added richness and creaminess. The ricotta will keep for up to 5 days stored airtight in the refrigerator.

MAKES: about 2 cups

4 cups whole milk
1 cup heavy cream
¾ cup buttermilk
1 tablespoon fresh lemon juice

1. In a large heavy pot, combine the milk, cream, buttermilk, and lemon juice and cook over medium heat, stirring occasionally to prevent scorching, for about 25 minutes, or until the mixture has reached 160°F. The mixture will begin to separate into milky cheese curds and a watery whey, which is the result you want.

2. Line a strainer with cheesecloth and set it over a bowl. Pour the milk mixture into the sieve and refrigerate for about 2 hours, or until most of the liquid has drained from the cheese. The texture of the cheese will depend on the draining time; for a firmer texture, drain the cheese for as long as overnight.

3. Remove the ricotta from the cheesecloth, transfer to an airtight container, and refrigerate until ready to use.

Chapter 3
SIDES

YOU WANT TO KNOW MY SECRET for a really awesome meal? It's pretty simple: the sides. With just a little effort, sides take a midweek dinner from just OK to a special occasion.

Although we can roast potatoes and steam green beans with ease, I'm all about taking classic side dishes to another level: "braising" spring vegetables in a chicken broth, creaming your own fresh summer corn, or baking puffy buttered buns from scratch are just some of the ways that you can add flavor, texture, and depth to a meal. Some of these recipes may sound a little fancy, but I promise you, they're easy to execute. I cook most of them while the casserole is baking in the oven or the pasta is boiling on the stovetop.

For a calm kitchen, I try to prep my ingredients in stages or during any spare moments I can grab—just 5 minutes of chopping, whisking up a dressing, or toasting nuts ahead of time makes a noticeable difference. This is especially so for more involved sides like My Favorite Potato Salad.

And to squeeze the most fun out of making all of these dishes, I call on my family "sous chefs," Linds and Hud or a couple of mates, for culinary backup. Cooking is so much more fun when others are around to help shell fava beans or chop shallots. Plus, when we sit down to our delicious little spread, everyone is proud of the food in front of us.

So, now that the sides are on the table, it's game time! Serving food family-style, passing plates of Crispy Potato Cakes, Butternut Squash with Sage and Brown Butter, and Peas with Rosemary-Parmesan Cream (to name a few) around the table, and serving one another creates a social atmosphere that you just don't get with an already assembled plate of "meat and three." You pretty quickly find out who is fussy, who's the greedy pig of the group, and who doesn't like spicy broccolini. It's kind of like a "get to know you" game at the table.

Sharing food this way puts guests at ease; they choose how much or how little ends up on their plate and if for some *craaazy* reason they are not a fan of one of your dishes or have an intolerance to certain ingredients, no drama—there's plenty more deliciousness to choose from on the table. So c'mon, how about a little something on the side?

Humble Beans

Give pinto beans a little love with this easy-to-make side. It calls for only a handful of ingredients, but the beans are enriched with the flavor of pork. (Of course, if you prefer vegetarian beans, just omit the pork.) You can take this simple dish to Italy by cooking the beans with a sprig of rosemary or to Mexico by finishing them with chopped chiles and cilantro. And because the beans will be tenderized in the pressure cooker, you don't need to soak them first.

SERVES: 8

PREP TIME: 5 minutes

COOK TIME: 1 hour and 35 minutes

MAKE-AHEAD: The beans can be made up to 3 days ahead, cooled, covered, and refrigerated. Reheat, covered, over medium heat.

1 tablespoon canola oil

1 8-ounce bone-in country-style pork rib or 8 ounces boneless pork shoulder

Kosher salt and freshly ground black pepper

1 large white onion, diced

1 pound dried pinto beans (about 2½ cups), picked over, rinsed, and drained

6 cups water

1. Heat a 6-quart pressure cooker over medium-high heat and add the oil. Season the pork with salt and pepper and cook, turning occasionally, for about 8 minutes, or until golden brown all over. Stir in the onion and sauté for about 4 minutes, or until golden brown. Stir in the beans and water.

2. Lock the pressure cooker lid in place and bring to high pressure over high heat, about 15 minutes. Reduce the heat to medium-low to stabilize the pressure and cook for 55 minutes. Remove from the heat and allow the pressure to subside on its own, about 20 minutes.

3. Unlock the pressure cooker and remove the lid, tilting it away from you to allow the steam to escape. The pork and beans will be very tender.

4. Remove the pork from the beans and pull it into bite-size pieces; discard the bone and cartilage. Return the meat to the pot. Season the beans and broth to taste with salt and pepper and serve.

VARIATION If you don't have a pressure cooker, this can be cooked in a pot in the traditional manner. Soak the beans in water for at least 12 hours. Drain the beans. In a large heavy pot over medium-high heat, heat the oil. Season the pork with salt and pepper and cook for about 8 minutes, or until golden brown all over. Stir in the onion and sauté for about 4 minutes, or until golden brown. Stir in the beans and water. Bring the mixture to a simmer and simmer gently for 1½ hours, or until the pork and beans are very tender. Continue as directed in step 4.

Grilled Eggplant with Mint Vinaigrette

SERVES: 4

PREP TIME: 20 minutes, plus 30 minutes for salting the eggplant

COOK TIME: 20 minutes

MAKE-AHEAD: The vinaigrette can be made up to 4 hours ahead, covered and refrigerated. Let stand at room temperature for 15 minutes and rewhisk to blend before using.

2 eggplants (1 pound each), cut crosswise into ½-inch-thick slices

Kosher salt

8 tablespoons extra-virgin olive oil

Freshly ground black pepper

1 lemon

2 tablespoons white wine vinegar

¼ cup finely chopped shallots

1 tablespoon finely chopped fresh mint, plus small leaves for garnish

A small square of feta cheese, for shaving

Eggplant's texture is spongy and unappetizing when raw, but when cooked properly, it becomes silky, creamy, and such a delight to eat. The fresh mint vinaigrette gives this dish a Mediterranean feel, making it an ideal accompaniment to Greek dishes. In the summer, when eggplants are abundant in the farmers' market, I like to use all different shapes, sizes, and colors.

1. Lay the eggplant slices in a single layer on two baking sheets and sprinkle both sides with salt. Set aside for about 30 minutes, or until moisture beads on top of the eggplant.

2. Prepare a grill for medium-high heat.

3. Rinse the eggplant to remove the excess salt and pat dry. Brush the eggplant slices with 3 tablespoons of the oil, coating both sides. Season with salt and pepper. Working in batches, grill the eggplant for about 5 minutes per side, or until char marks form and the eggplant is very tender. Transfer to a platter as you finish each batch.

4. Meanwhile, grate the zest of the lemon into a small bowl. Halve the lemon and squeeze 2 tablespoons of juice into the bowl. Whisk in the vinegar, shallots, chopped mint, and the remaining 5 tablespoons oil. Season the vinaigrette to taste with salt and pepper.

5. Spoon the vinaigrette over the grilled eggplant and sprinkle with the mint leaves. Using a vegetable peeler, shave thin slices of cheese over the eggplant. Sprinkle with pepper and serve.

WHY SALT EGGPLANT?

Salting the eggplant draws out bitterness. It also draws out water, which you can see happening moments after salting it. Removing excess moisture helps give the cooked eggplant a creamy, silken texture.

Creamed Corn

Throw everything you know about creamed corn out the window, because this fresh version is incomparable. The corn, which is very quickly sautéed, pops with sweetness and is complemented by the silky sauce. Serve this rich, indulgent side with everything from grilled steak to grilled whole fish.

SERVES: 4

PREP TIME: 10 minutes

COOK TIME: 8 minutes

2 tablespoons (¼ stick) unsalted butter

1 medium onion, finely chopped (1 cup)

8 fresh thyme sprigs

6 ears yellow corn, shucked and kernels cut off

1 cup heavy cream

½ cup whole milk

Kosher salt and freshly ground black pepper

1. In a large nonstick skillet, melt the butter over medium heat. Add the onion and thyme and sauté for about 4 minutes, or until the onion is tender and very pale golden. Stir in the corn, then stir in the cream and milk, bring to a simmer, and simmer for about 3 minutes, or until the corn is heated through but still crisp-tender.

2. Season the corn to taste with salt and pepper. Discard the thyme stems and serve immediately.

ON THE LIGHTER SIDE

If you're looking for a leaner corn side dish, simply sauté some finely chopped shallots in oil until tender, then add a sprig of thyme, stir in the corn, and cook for about 3 minutes, or until the corn is crisp-tender. You'll get that nice crunch of corn and a beautiful color to brighten up the table.

Pan-Roasted Brussels Sprouts with Chorizo

SERVES: 4

PREP TIME: 20 minutes

COOK TIME: 20 minutes

MAKE-AHEAD: The Brussels sprouts can be prepped and the chorizo diced up to 4 hours ahead, covered, and refrigerated.

1 teaspoon caraway seeds

2 tablespoons olive oil

1½ pounds Brussels sprouts (about 20 medium), halved and tough outer leaves removed

2 scallions, trimmed and thinly sliced

⅓ cup diced Spanish chorizo

Kosher salt and freshly ground black pepper

Brussels sprouts are an underdog vegetable that have recently risen up the ranks to become a cult culinary hero. In this dish, the smokiness of the chorizo and the rye flavor of the caraway seeds play against the caramelized sprouts to extraordinary effect. Serve with the Roasted Pork Belly with Homemade Applesauce (page 55) or Simple Roast Chicken and Potatoes (page 48) for a delicious meal.

 If you want to double the recipe, make sure you use two pans so the sprouts aren't crowded and will caramelize rather than steam.

---

1. In a small heavy skillet, stir the caraway seeds over medium heat for about 2 minutes, or until toasted and fragrant. Transfer the seeds to a spice grinder or mortar and pestle and grind to a powder.

2. Heat a large heavy skillet over medium heat. Add the oil, then add the Brussels sprouts, scallions, and chorizo and sauté for about 5 minutes, or until the Brussels sprouts are tender and beginning to caramelize. Mix in the ground caraway. Season to taste with salt and pepper and serve immediately.

Butternut Squash with Sage and Brown Butter

SERVES: 6

PREP TIME: 10 minutes

COOK TIME: 35 minutes

MAKE-AHEAD: The butternut squash can be cut up to 6 hours ahead, covered and refrigerated.

2 butternut squash (about 1 pound each), peeled, halved, seeded, and cut into 2-inch cubes

2 tablespoons olive oil

Kosher salt and freshly ground black pepper

4 tablespoons (½ stick) unsalted butter, diced

¼ cup thinly sliced fresh sage leaves

3 tablespoons toasted shelled pumpkin seeds (pepitas)

¼ cup shaved Parmesan cheese

Squash is super-adaptable—it can star in anything from pasta fillings to soups—and its sweet flavor and silky texture make it a definite crowd-pleaser. This roasted squash is delicious with Parm-Crusted Pork Chops with Lemony Kale Salad (page 57).

1. Preheat the oven 450°F.

2. On a large heavy baking sheet, toss the squash with the oil to coat and season with salt and pepper. Scatter the butter over the squash. Roast the squash for about 20 minutes, or until it begins to soften and turn golden brown.

3. Scatter the sage over the squash and toss well. Continue roasting for about 15 minutes, or until the squash is tender and well caramelized. Season to taste with salt and pepper.

4. Divide the squash among six plates, sprinkle with the pumpkin seeds and cheese, and serve immediately.

My Favorite Potato Salad

Here's the twist that takes this potato salad from everyday to extra-special: the warm boiled potatoes are pumped up with rich flavor when they're tossed with hot chicken broth that is flavored with shallots, cornichons, and capers. I think of this salad as a bit of a wingman because I take it everywhere with me, and it never fails me at picnics, BBQs, or at my own dinner table. A great side for Maple-Glazed Planked Salmon (page 85), or anything from the grill.

1. Place the potatoes in a large saucepan of salted water, bring the water to a boil over medium-high heat, and boil for about 10 minutes, or until the potatoes are just tender; a sharp knife should pierce a piece of potato easily and the potato should slip off the knife without falling apart.

2. Meanwhile, in a large heavy nonstick skillet, cook the bacon over medium-high heat for about 6 minutes, or until crisp and golden brown. Transfer the bacon to a plate lined with paper towels to drain.

3. In a small saucepan, bring the broth to a simmer over high heat. Add the shallots, cornichons, and capers, reduce the heat to medium-low, and simmer very gently for 2 to 3 minutes, or until the shallots soften slightly. Remove from the heat.

4. Drain the potatoes in a colander and gently shake them to release excess moisture. Transfer the potatoes to a large bowl.

5. Add one-third of the broth mixture to the hot potatoes and, using a silicone spatula, gently fold and turn the potatoes in the hot broth for about 2 minutes, or until most of it has been absorbed. Repeat 2 more times, adding all of the solids and just enough of the broth to moisten. The potatoes should break down a bit. Set aside.

6. Gently fold the bacon and parsley into the warm potatoes, then gently fold in the aïoli. Season to taste with salt and pepper. Serve warm, at room temperature, or chilled.

SERVES: 8

PREP TIME: 20 minutes

COOK TIME: 20 minutes

MAKE-AHEAD: The potato salad is best when it is still warm, but it can be made up to 8 hours ahead, covered, and refrigerated, then served cold or at room temperature.

4 pounds Yukon gold potatoes, peeled and cut into 1½-inch chunks

Kosher salt

8 ounces bacon (about 8 slices), finely diced

1½ cups low-sodium chicken broth

2 medium shallots, finely chopped (½ cup)

⅓ cup finely chopped cornichons

¼ cup drained capers

¼ cup finely chopped fresh flat-leaf parsley

⅓ cup Aïoli (page 30) or mayonnaise

Freshly ground black pepper

Roasted Romanesco and Carrots with Tarragon Sauce

SERVES: 4

PREP TIME: 20 minutes

COOK TIME: 25 minutes

12 ounces medium carrots (preferably heirloom; about 8), peeled, trimmed, and halved lengthwise

12 ounces romanesco or cauliflower (about 1 small head), separated into 2-inch florets (with 1-inch-long stems)

6 small shallots, peeled and halved

¼ cup olive oil

Kosher salt and freshly ground black pepper

2 ½-inch-thick slices ciabatta bread, crusts removed

¼ cup red wine vinegar

½ cup extra-virgin olive oil

⅓ cup finely chopped fresh tarragon

2 tablespoons finely chopped fresh flat-leaf parsley

1 garlic clove, finely chopped

Romanesco, cauliflower's magical-looking green cousin, is becoming more readily available. It's worth seeking out for its earthy flavor and craggy florets, but if you can't find it, you can substitute cauliflower. Here I drizzle roasted romanesco and heirloom carrots with an Italian tarragon or "dragoncello" sauce—an herbaceous sauce made with vinegar-soaked ciabatta bread. Serve with Porcini-Braised Beef with Horseradish Mascarpone (page 65) or Simple Roast Chicken and Potatoes (page 48).

1. Position a rack in the center of the oven and place a large heavy baking sheet on the rack. Preheat the oven to 425°F.

2. In a large bowl, toss the carrots, romanesco, and shallots with the olive oil to coat. Season with salt and pepper. Spread the vegetables out on the preheated baking sheet and roast, stirring occasionally, for about 25 minutes, or until tender and deeply browned all over.

3. Meanwhile, put the bread in a small bowl, pour the vinegar over it, and soak for 5 minutes.

4. Squeeze the excess vinegar out of the bread and discard the vinegar, then return the bread to the bowl and break it up as finely as possible. Add the extra-virgin olive oil, tarragon, parsley, and garlic and stir to combine. Season to taste with salt.

5. Transfer the roasted vegetables to a platter. Drizzle the tarragon sauce over and serve immediately.

Quick-Braised Spring Vegetables

Quickly "braising" your veggies with spring onion, garlic, olive oil, and a few tablespoons of chicken broth adds bucketloads of flavor to them, as does a good sprinkling of chives and grated Parmesan. I can't wait to whip up this spring dish after a visit to the farmers' market—it's a testament to the season.

SERVES: 6

PREP TIME: 10 minutes

COOK TIME: 6 minutes

1. In a large heavy skillet, combine the spring onion, garlic, oil, and broth and bring to a simmer over medium heat. Cover and cook for about 2 minutes, or until the spring onion softens slightly.

2. Add the asparagus, fava beans, and peas and sauté for about 2 minutes, or until the beans and peas are heated through. Add the escarole, spinach, and basil and sauté for about 2 minutes, or until the escarole wilts and the asparagus is crisp-tender.

3. Stir in the lemon zest and juice. Season to taste with salt. Transfer to a serving platter. Sprinkle with the chives, grate the Parmesan over, and serve immediately.

1 spring onion or 4 scallions, trimmed and sliced

2 garlic cloves, finely chopped

3 tablespoons olive oil

3 tablespoons low-sodium chicken broth or water

8 ounces asparagus, woody ends trimmed, stalks cut into 1½-inch pieces

1 cup shelled fresh fava beans (from about 1 pound pods), peeled (see Note), or sugar snap peas, trimmed and halved crosswise

1 cup shelled fresh English peas (from about 1 pound peas in the pod)

½ head escarole, torn into bite-size pieces (about 2 cups)

3 cups loosely packed baby spinach leaves

½ cup loosely packed fresh basil leaves

1 tablespoon grated lemon zest

1 tablespoon fresh lemon juice

Kosher salt

1 tablespoon finely chopped fresh chives

A small chunk of Parmesan cheese, for grating

FAVA BEANS PREP

Fava beans have an inedible pod and an outer skin that is only edible when the beans are very young. To prepare fava beans, remove the beans from the pods. Next, bring a large pot of water to a boil. Add the beans and cook for 30 seconds. Immediately transfer the beans to a bowl of ice water. When chilled, drain the beans and, using your fingers or a small knife, peel the outer skins from the beans.

Jasmine Rice

SERVES: 4

PREP TIME: 5 minutes

COOK TIME: 20 minutes

1 cup jasmine rice

1½ cups water

¾ teaspoon kosher salt

Fragrant jasmine rice can round out a meal and soaks up spicy Asian sauces. Rinse it carefully and be sure to let the cooked rice stand briefly before serving for the fluffiest result. You can use this same method to cook basmati rice.

---

1. Put the rice in a sieve and rinse under cold running water, stirring the rice with your hand, until the water runs fairly clear. Drain well.

2. In a small heavy saucepan, bring the rice, water, and salt to a boil over high heat. Reduce the heat to low, cover, and simmer gently for about 15 minutes, or until the water has been absorbed and the rice is tender. (Don't stir the rice during cooking, as this can release starches that cause sticking.)

3. Fluff the rice with a fork and let stand, covered, for 5 minutes before serving.

Spicy Broccolini Fried Rice

A cross between broccoli and Chinese kale, broccolini has long, tender stalks and a slightly sweeter flavor than broccoli. Stir-fry this bright green vegetable with garlic, ginger, chile, scallions, and cooked Jasmine Rice (page 128) for a Chinese side to pair with Maple-Glazed Planked Salmon (page 85), Teriyaki Beef Ribs with Enoki Mushrooms (page 73), Roasted Pork Belly with Homemade Applesauce (page 55), or Whole Grilled Branzino with Soy-Ginger Sauce (page 89). You can also swap out the broccolini for broccoli, sugar snap peas, snow peas, or asparagus. How's that for versatile?

---

1. Heat a heavy wok or large heavy skillet over medium-high heat and add the oil. When a wisp of smoke rises from the pan, add the garlic, ginger, chile, and sliced scallion whites and stir-fry for 1 minute, or until fragrant. Add the broccolini and 1 tablespoon of the soy sauce and cook, stir-frying, for 1½ minutes, or until the broccolini is crisp-tender.

2. Add the rice and the remaining 1 tablespoon soy sauce and cook, stir-frying, for 2 minutes, or until the rice is heated through. Stir in the scallion greens.

3. Transfer the rice to a platter, sprinkle with the sesame seeds, and serve immediately.

SERVES: 4

PREP TIME: 5 minutes

COOK TIME: 5 minutes

MAKE-AHEAD: The vegetables can be cut up to 2 hours ahead, covered and refrigerated.

1 tablespoon coconut oil or grapeseed oil

1 tablespoon finely chopped garlic

1 tablespoon finely chopped peeled fresh ginger

1 small Fresno chile, seeded and finely chopped

2 scallions, trimmed and thinly sliced, white and green parts kept separate

1 bunch broccolini, trimmed, florets cut into ½-inch pieces and stems sliced

2 tablespoons soy sauce

2 cups cold Jasmine Rice (page 128)

1 teaspoon black sesame seeds (see Note)

BLACK SESAME SEEDS

These seeds contrast beautifully with the rice and add a distinctive flavor. You can find black sesame seeds in most Asian grocery stores and specialty food shops. If you can't find them, just use toasted white sesame seeds instead.

Peas with Rosemary-Parmesan Cream

SERVES: 4

PREP TIME: 10 minutes

COOK TIME: 10 minutes

MAKE-AHEAD: The peas can be boiled up to 1 day ahead. Submerge them in ice water when they come out of the boiling water until they are cool, then drain well, cover, and refrigerate.

3 cups fresh peas (from about
3 pounds peas in the pod)

½ cup heavy cream

1 small fresh rosemary sprig

2 tablespoons (¼ stick) unsalted butter

¼ cup finely grated Parmesan cheese

Freshly ground black pepper

With their antioxidants, sweet taste, and beautiful color, peas are nutritional powerhouses and stars at the dinner table. Here I fold them into a rich Parmesan cream for a side to serve with Simple Roast Chicken and Potatoes (page 48), Roasted Pork Belly with Homemade Applesauce (page 55), Porcini-Braised Beef with Horseradish Mascarpone (page 65), or Meat Pies (page 71). Don't get me wrong, I love the classic English pairing of meat pies with mushy peas—but these creamy, crisp-tender peas give the mushy stuff a good run for its money.

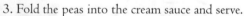

1. In a large saucepan of boiling salted water, cook the peas for about 4 minutes, or until they are just tender. Drain well.

2. Meanwhile, in a medium heavy saucepan, combine the cream and rosemary and cook over medium heat, whisking, for about 2 minutes, or until the cream begins to bubble slightly. Whisk in the butter until melted, then whisk in the cheese. Season to taste with pepper. Discard the rosemary sprig.

3. Fold the peas into the cream sauce and serve.

Green Bean and Cherry Tomato Gratin

Here you get everything you love about a gratin in a healthy green bean dish. With juicy cherry tomatoes and a buttery macadamia nut–panko crust, this gratin is a treat for your taste buds. Gratins feed many mouths and are served up family-style straight from the baking dish, which means the food stays nice 'n' hot.

1. Preheat the oven to 400°F.

2. In a food processor, pulse the nuts for 10 seconds, or until they resemble fine crumbs. In a medium bowl, mix the nuts, panko, and 2 tablespoons of the olive oil. Spread the mixture on a small baking sheet and toast in the oven, stirring occasionally, for about 4 minutes, or until golden. Set aside.

3. Meanwhile, bring a large saucepan of water to a boil over high heat. Add the beans and cook for about 4 minutes, or until bright green and just tender. Drain and transfer the beans to a large bowl of ice water to cool completely, then drain well, pat dry, and transfer to a large bowl.

4. Heat a medium saucepan over medium-low heat. Add the remaining 1 tablespoon olive oil, then add the shallots and sauté for about 2 minutes, or until tender and pale golden. Add the capers and lemon zest and cook for about 2 minutes, or until fragrant. Stir in the extra-virgin olive oil and lemon juice, then add the cherry tomatoes.

5. Add the tomato mixture to the green beans. Season with salt and pepper, and gently toss to mix. Transfer the mixture to a 9-inch baking dish. Sprinkle the bread crumb mixture over the top.

6. Bake the gratin for about 12 minutes, or until heated through. Serve.

SERVES: 8

PREP TIME: 15 minutes

COOK TIME: 25 minutes

MAKE-AHEAD: The recipe can be prepared through step 3 up to 1 day ahead. Cover separately and refrigerate, then proceed with step 4 when ready to assemble and bake the gratin.

½ cup macadamia nuts

½ cup panko (Japanese dried bread crumbs; see Note)

3 tablespoons olive oil

1½ pounds green beans, ends trimmed and cut diagonally in half

3 medium shallots, thinly sliced (¾ cup)

2 tablespoons drained capers

1½ teaspoons finely grated lemon zest

⅓ cup extra-virgin olive oil

2 tablespoons fresh lemon juice

1 pound cherry tomatoes, halved

Kosher salt and freshly ground black pepper

PANKO

Panko crumbs are dried Japanese bread crumbs made from bread without crusts; hence their white color. Their large, light flakes don't absorb much grease and give foods a long-lasting crunchy coating.

Crispy Potato Cakes

SERVES: 6

PREP TIME: 15 minutes, plus 1 hour for chilling

COOK TIME: 35 minutes

MAKE-AHEAD: The potato sheet can be made up to 1 day ahead, covered, and refrigerated.

4 medium russet (baking) potatoes (about 8 ounces each)

4 scallions, trimmed and finely chopped

1 tablespoon cornstarch

2 teaspoons fresh thyme leaves

1 teaspoon kosher salt

4 tablespoons canola oil

2 tablespoons (¼ stick) unsalted butter

Don't hesitate to switch up your usual potato routine with this crispy spin-off. Pair these cakes with Porcini-Braised Beef with Horseradish Mascarpone (page 65) or Roasted Pork Belly with Homemade Applesauce (page 55) for a no-holds-barred dinner. I also like these guys with big egg dishes in the morning, like Poached Eggs with Bacon, Avocado, and Lime Mojo (page 195).

1. Bring a large pot of salted water to a boil over high heat. Add the potatoes and cook for about 15 minutes, or until they are soft on the outside but still firm in the center. Drain the potatoes and cool slightly.

2. With a small knife, peel the warm potatoes.

3. Using the large holes on a box grater, shred the still-warm potatoes into a large bowl. Add the scallions, cornstarch, thyme, and salt and toss well.

4. Line a small baking sheet (12 x 9 inches) with parchment paper or plastic wrap. Press the potato mixture evenly over the baking sheet, forming a ½-inch-thick layer. Top with another sheet of parchment paper or plastic wrap and refrigerate for at least 1 hour, or until cold and set.

5. Preheat the oven to 200°F. Place a nonstick baking sheet in the oven.

6. Remove the potato sheet from the baking pan and cut it lengthwise in half, then cut each half into 6 rectangles, for a total of 12 rectangles.

7. In a large heavy nonstick skillet, heat 2 tablespoons of the oil over medium-high heat. Place 6 potato cakes in the pan and cook for about 4 minutes, or until crisp and golden brown on the bottom. Add 1 tablespoon of the butter and cook until melted. Turn the potato cakes over and continue cooking until crisp and golden brown on the bottom and heated through. Transfer to paper towels to drain any excess oil. Keep warm in the oven while making the remaining potato cakes. Wipe the skillet out and repeat with the remaining 2 tablespoons oil, potato cakes, and butter. Transfer the potato cakes to a platter and serve immediately.

Cheddar-and-Corn Cream Biscuits

MAKES: 6 biscuits

PREP TIME: 10 minutes

COOK TIME: 20 minutes

MAKE-AHEAD: These biscuits are best
served as soon as they are baked, but if they
aren't all devoured right away, you can store
them airtight at room temperature for up to
1 day, then rewarm them in a 350°F oven.

1½ cups all-purpose flour

1½ teaspoons baking powder

1½ teaspoons sugar

1 teaspoon kosher salt

1 cup shredded white Cheddar cheese
(about 3 ounces)

⅓ cup fresh corn kernels

1⅓ cups chilled heavy cream

Corn becomes even more delicious when it mingles with savory white
Cheddar, and it's especially the case with these summery biscuits. Use
your hands or a wooden spoon to mix the ingredients very gently,
which will give the biscuits a desirable tender texture. If you want to
make these off season, just leave out the corn—you won't get any
complaints. Serve with barbecued ribs or Homemade Chicken Soup
Makes Me Feel Better (page 19).

1. Preheat the oven to 425°F. Line a baking sheet with parchment paper.

2. In a large bowl, whisk the flour, baking powder, sugar, and salt to blend.
   Using your hands or a wooden spoon, mix in the cheese and corn. Add
   the cream and gently mix with your hands or a wooden spoon just until
   a moist dough forms; do not overwork or knead the dough, or the
   biscuits will be tough.

3. Form the dough into 6 mounds on the prepared baking sheet, spacing
   them evenly. Bake for about 20 minutes, or until the biscuits are golden
   brown on the top and bottom and just baked through. Serve warm.

Buttered Buns

These billowy buns are a great introduction to baking your own yeast breads because they're simple but special. Plus they're great for sandwich fillings. Hudson and I have fun rolling out the dough, though the kitchen looks like a flour-bomb has hit it when we're done. Add extra flavor to the buns by sprinkling poppy or sesame seeds over them just before they go into the oven.

1. In a small bowl, whisk the yeast and warm water together. Let stand for 10 minutes, or until foamy.

2. In a small saucepan, stir the milk and shortening over medium-low heat just until most of the shortening has melted and the mixture is lukewarm. Transfer to a large bowl.

3. Stir the sugar and salt into the milk mixture. Whisk in the egg, then whisk in the yeast mixture. Add the flour and stir until the dough forms. Transfer the dough to a lightly floured surface and knead for about 5 minutes, or until smooth.

4. Transfer the dough to a lightly oiled bowl and turn it to coat with oil. Cover loosely with plastic wrap and let rise in a warm, draft-free area for about 1 hour, or until doubled in size. (Alternatively, you can refrigerate the dough for up to 1 day to rise slowly.)

5. Brush two 8-inch round or square cake pans or baking dishes with some of the melted butter. Punch the dough down and divide it into 14 equal pieces (about 2 ounces each). Roll each piece into a ball: Lightly moisten the work surface with water so the dough sticks to the surface slightly and pulls as you are cupping it with your hand to shape it. Don't feel as if you have to have perfectly shaped buns—the buns are actually most attractive when a little rustic and bumpy.

6. Arrange 7 dough balls in each of the prepared pans and brush generously with melted butter. Cover and let rise in a warm, draft-free area for about 30 minutes, or until the buns just begin to touch. (Reserve the remaining melted butter.)

7. Preheat the oven to 350°F.

8. Bake the buns for about 16 minutes, or until they are puffed and golden brown. While the buns bake, remelt the reserved butter. Brush the warm buns generously with the melted butter and serve warm.

MAKES: 14 buns

PREP TIME: 30 minutes, plus about 1½ hours for the dough to rise

COOK TIME: 16 minutes

MAKE-AHEAD: These buns are at their best when freshly baked, but they can be baked up to 1 day ahead, cooled, and stored airtight at room temperature. To reheat the buns, wrap them in aluminum foil and warm in a 375°F oven for about 5 minutes, or until heated through.

1 envelope active dry yeast

⅓ cup warm water (110° to 115°F)

1 cup whole milk

¼ cup nonhydrogenated vegetable shortening

3 tablespoons sugar

1½ teaspoons kosher salt

1 large egg

3⅔ cups all-purpose flour

6 tablespoons (¾ stick) salted butter, melted

Chapter 4
SWEETS

———

"HIDE YOUR CHOCOLATES! Curtis is coming. . . ." I'm quite like a tornado when it comes to anything sweet. I swoop up whatever is in sight, leaving only a trail of crumbs in my path. Even my own freezer isn't safe, with fresh mint gelato and lime granita being wiped out nearly as quickly as they're made.

As far as desserts go, I enjoy the process of making them almost as much as I love inhaling them . . . almost. After making more soufflés than I care to remember in my restaurants and at home, I still get a kick out of watching them puff up and rise proudly out of their little ramekins as they bake. I'm typically a chocolate soufflé kind of guy, but the Roasted Banana Soufflés with Caramel Sauce threaten to knock that widely loved classic right off its perch. The sauce is a totally decadent add-on here, but why not? Bananas + caramel = bloody awesome combo!

And while I'm in the mood for sweet confessions, I blame (or thank? I haven't quite decided yet) my mum for all of this, because she used to let me sit on the kitchen counter and lick the beaters once she'd finished making brownies or eat cookie dough straight from the rubber spatula in all of its raw sugary and buttery glory. Watching my mum bake; anticipating the cakes, muffins, Pavlovas, tarts, and pies that would be coming out of the oven; and breathing in those sweet and comforting aromas—these are all beautiful memories. I've created my own take on each of those classic dishes and more in this chapter. Let me tell you, if you want your family to smile from ear to ear on a Sunday night, all you need to do is make the bubbling Cherry-Amaretto Lattice Pie. Or, if you're after something super-quick but equally rewarding, try the winter citrus tart. Friends are always blown away when I bring this one to the table, with its dusting of confectioners' sugar and side of rosemary whipped cream.

When it comes to desserts, I don't cut any delicious corners—I go for it! I urge you to dive in too.

Cherry-Amaretto Lattice Pie

Pull this cherry pie out of your back pocket for your next special summer occasion or Sunday night family meal. The pie looks like something from the best pastry shop in town but is far better than any store-bought dessert. The cherries are fresh, the dough is super buttery and tender, and the lattice allows steam to escape, thickening the juices and concentrating the flavor of the pie filling.

SERVES: 8 to 10

PREP TIME: 30 minutes

COOK TIME: 1 hour and 20 minutes, plus at least 1 hour cooling time

MAKE-AHEAD: The pie is best served warm but it will keep, covered, at room temperature, for up to 1 day.

1. Position one rack in the lower third of the oven and a second rack just above it. Set a baking sheet on the bottom rack. (Being near the heat source will help the bottom crust bake and brown properly. The baking sheet will catch any bubbled-over juices.) Preheat the oven to 425°F.

2. In a medium bowl, combine ¾ cup of the sugar, the cornstarch, and the salt. Stir in the cherries, amaretto, lemon juice, and cinnamon stick; set aside.

3. Unwrap the larger disk of dough, set it on a floured surface, and lightly dust the top of the dough. Roll out the dough into a 13-inch round, occasionally rotating the dough and dusting it with flour to prevent sticking. Brush away the excess flour and transfer the dough to a 9½-inch glass pie plate, centering it in the pie plate and letting the excess dough hang over the edges. Lightly press the dough into the dish. Refrigerate the pie shell.

4. On the floured surface, roll out the other disk of dough into a 12-inch round. Using a large knife, cut ten 1-inch-wide strips from the dough round.

5. Transfer the cherry filling to the pie shell, then scatter the butter on top. Arrange the dough strips over the filling, forming a lattice (see Note on page 146). Trim the dough overhang to ¾ inch. Pinch the bottom crust and strips together and fold the overhang under. Crimp the edges to seal. Lightly brush the lattice with the milk and sprinkle the remaining 2 teaspoons sugar over it.

¾ cup plus 2 teaspoons sugar

3 tablespoons cornstarch

¼ teaspoon salt

5 cups pitted fresh dark sweet cherries (about 2 pounds unpitted cherries)

¼ cup amaretto

2 tablespoons fresh lemon juice

1 cinnamon stick

Buttery Pastry Dough (recipe follows), shaped into 2 disks and chilled

1 tablespoon unsalted butter, cut into ½-inch cubes

1½ teaspoons whole milk

Vanilla ice cream, for serving

(continued)

6. Bake the pie on the rack above the baking sheet for 20 minutes. Reduce the oven temperature to 350°F and bake the pie for about 1 hour longer, or until the crust is deep golden and the filling is bubbling. If the crust begins to brown too quickly, tent the pie with foil. Let the pie cool on a wire rack until warm, about 1 hour.

7. Cut the pie into wedges and serve warm with ice cream.

HOW TO LATTICE

The word "lattice" refers to the strips of pastry woven together to create the top crust. Once you get going, latticing is a pretty simple technique, and it's fun to do. If weaving feels a bit intimidating, though, just lay half of the strips across the pie parallel to each other, then lay the remaining strips across them, perpendicular to the bottom strips. Don't worry if your strips aren't perfect— all the more handmade charm.

Here's how to form a woven lattice: Lay half of the strips across the filling, spacing them evenly. Fold back every other strip; then place another strip perpendicular at the folded edge of the strips. Unfold the folded strips so they lie over the perpendicular strip. Fold back the other set of strips. Stopping about 1 inch from the first perpendicular strip, place a second perpendicular strip at the folds, and unfold the folded strips. Repeat with the remaining 3 pastry strips to cover the pie with the lattice.

Buttery Pastry Dough

The secret to homemade pastry dough is to avoid blitzing your butter to smithereens in the food processor. Leaving pea-size pieces of butter in the dough is key, because they will melt in the oven and release water, which will become steam. The steam helps to puff up the dough and contributes to that melt-in-your-mouth texture. The dough can be made up to 1 day ahead, covered, and refrigerated. Alternatively, it can be frozen for up to 1 month.

MAKES: Enough for one 2-crust pie or 12 individual pies

2½ cups all-purpose flour
1 tablespoon sugar
½ teaspoon fine sea salt or table salt
½ pound (2 sticks) cold unsalted butter, cut into ½-inch cubes
About ⅓ cup ice water

1. In a food processor, combine the flour, sugar, and salt and pulse to blend. Add the butter and pulse about 10 times, or until the butter is in pea-size pieces; do not overprocess. While pulsing the processor, add ⅓ cup of the ice water, then pulse just until moist clumps of dough form, adding more water 1 tablespoon at a time if necessary.

2. Transfer the dough to a work surface and divide it in half. If making the Cherry-Amaretto Lattice Pie (page 145), make one half slightly larger and shape each piece into a thick disk. If making the Meat Pies (page 71), divide each piece of dough into 6 pieces and shape into disks. Wrap individually in plastic wrap and refrigerate for at least 30 minutes before rolling out.

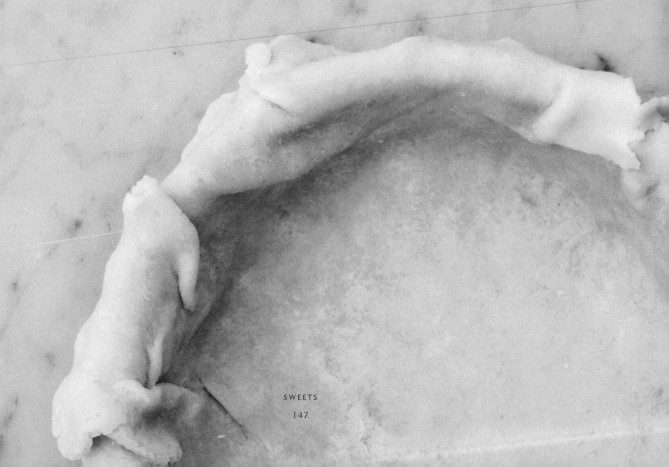

Winter Citrus Tart with Rosemary Whipped Cream

I have a huge soft spot for this dish. It requires very little labor for full-on flavor and is incredible to look at from the moment you arrange the sliced citrus fruit over the pastry, and becomes more and more delicious to the eye as it bakes: the pastry puffs up and turns golden and the oven heat deepens the color of the citrus. While an herbed whipped cream may sound unusual, it cuts through the fruit's sweetness and brings warmth to the dessert. Vanilla ice cream tastes pretty great with the warm tart too.

SERVES: 6

PREP TIME: 5 minutes

COOK TIME: 20 minutes

MAKE-AHEAD: The whipped cream can be made up to 4 hours ahead, covered, and refrigerated. Rewhip it lightly before serving.

2 oranges (navel, Cara Cara, or blood oranges), tangerines, or tangelos

1 9 x 9-inch sheet frozen puff pastry, thawed but still very cold

⅓ cup orange marmalade

¾ cup heavy cream

1 tablespoon powdered sugar, plus more for dusting

¼ teaspoon minced fresh rosemary

1. Preheat the oven to 425°F. Line a baking sheet with parchment paper.

2. Using a sharp knife, remove the peel and all the bitter white pith from the oranges. Slice each orange into about 8 thin slices.

3. Lay the pastry on the prepared baking sheet. Spread the marmalade over the pastry, leaving a 1-inch border around the edges. Arrange the orange slices on top, turning to coat them with the marmalade as you go.

4. Bake the tart for about 20 minutes, or until the pastry is a dark golden brown and cooked through. Halfway through baking, use a pastry brush to brush any juices from the oranges that have accumulated in the center over the pastry edges.

5. Meanwhile, in a medium bowl, whip the cream with the powdered sugar and the rosemary until thickened. Refrigerate until ready to serve.

6. After you remove the tart from the oven, brush any more accumulated juices over the oranges and pastry edges. Lightly dust the top of the tart with powdered sugar. Cut the tart into squares and serve warm with the cream.

Rum Pound Cake with Lime Glaze

SERVES: 12

PREP TIME: 20 minutes, plus 40 minutes cooling time

COOK TIME: 1 hour

MAKE-AHEAD: Leftovers will keep for up to 2 days, covered and stored at room temperature.

1⅓ cups all-purpose flour

¼ teaspoon baking powder

⅓ cup buttermilk

5 tablespoons golden rum

12 tablespoons (1½ sticks) unsalted butter, at room temperature

1¼ cups granulated sugar

¾ teaspoon pure vanilla extract

½ teaspoon salt

3 large eggs

Nonstick vegetable oil cooking spray

1¾ cups sifted powdered sugar

1½ tablespoons grated lime zest

3 tablespoons fresh lime juice

Rum and lime are a dream-team pair that injects this cake with zesty personality. The buttery crumb soaks up the lime glaze nicely so be sure to spoon it all over the freshly baked cake for a truly tasty result. Pound it!

1. Position a rack in the center of the oven and preheat the oven to 350°F.

2. In a medium bowl, whisk the flour and baking powder to blend. In a small bowl, combine the buttermilk and 4 tablespoons of the rum. In the bowl of a stand mixer fitted with the paddle attachment, beat the butter, granulated sugar, vanilla, and salt on medium-high speed for about 6 minutes, or until light and fluffy. Add the eggs one at a time, beating well after each addition. Reduce the speed to low and add the flour mixture and rum-buttermilk mixture alternately in three batches, beating just until blended.

3. Spray an 8-cup Kugelhopf (see Note) or Bundt pan with cooking spray. Scrape the batter into the prepared pan and bake for about 1 hour, or until a toothpick inserted near the center of the cake comes out with just a few moist crumbs attached. Cool on a cooling rack for 10 minutes, then invert the cake onto a plate or platter, remove the pan, and cool for about 30 minutes.

4. In a medium bowl, whisk the powdered sugar, lime zest and juice, and remaining 1 tablespoon rum until smooth. Spoon the glaze over the warm cake to coat. Serve the cake warm or at room temperature.

GRANNY'S PAN

I bake my pound cakes in my grandmum's Kugelhopf pan, which is similar to a Bundt pan, only smaller. There is something nice and old school about them, but you can also bake this cake in a 9 x 5-inch loaf pan. If you're using a Kugelhopf or Bundt pan, spray it with the nonstick cooking spray just before you transfer the batter to it, so that the spray doesn't have a chance to run down the sides and collect at the bottom.

Wedding Carrot Cupcakes with Brown Sugar Cream Cheese Frosting

Lindsay's favorite cake is carrot cake, so I baked her a big, beautiful one for our wedding in 2013. I know, I know . . . I'm a bit of a pathetic romantic when it comes to my girl. Not only did it make her swoon, but it tasted bloody delicious too. I'm now sharing the love with you guys in the form of cupcakes.

1. To make the cupcakes, preheat the oven to 350°F. Line 12 muffin cups with paper liners.

2. In a medium bowl, whisk the flour, baking powder, cinnamon, and salt to blend; set aside. In a large bowl, whisk the granulated sugar, eggs, and vanilla to blend. Slowly add the oil, whisking to blend well. Using a wooden spoon, stir in the flour mixture. Using a rubber spatula, fold in the carrots, raisins, and walnuts.

3. Divide the batter among the prepared muffin cups, using about ¼ cup batter for each cupcake. Bake for about 20 minutes, or until a toothpick inserted in the center of a cupcake comes out with just a few moist crumbs attached. Transfer the pan to a cooling rack and cool for 10 minutes, then transfer the cupcakes to the rack and cool completely.

4. To make the frosting, in the bowl of a stand mixer fitted with the paddle attachment (or in a large bowl, using a handheld mixer), beat the brown sugar, cream cheese, butter, and vanilla on medium speed for about 6 minutes, or until smooth, fluffy, and creamy.

5. Spread the frosting over the tops of the cupcakes.

MAKES: 12 cupcakes

PREP TIME: 15 minutes, plus about 30 minutes cooling time

COOK TIME: 20 minutes

MAKE-AHEAD: The frosted cupcakes will keep for up to 2 days, stored airtight in the refrigerator. Serve the cupcakes cold or at room temperature.

CUPCAKES

1 cup all-purpose flour

1 teaspoon baking powder

1 teaspoon ground cinnamon

½ teaspoon kosher salt

1 cup granulated sugar

2 large eggs

1 teaspoon pure vanilla extract

¾ cup canola oil

10 ounces carrots (about 3), coarsely grated on a box grater

½ cup golden raisins

½ cup walnuts, coarsely chopped

FROSTING

¾ cup packed light brown sugar

1 8-ounce package cream cheese, at room temperature

3 tablespoons unsalted butter, at room temperature

½ teaspoon pure vanilla extract

Bittersweet Chocolate Sabayon with Fresh Raspberries and Whipped Crème Fraîche

SERVES: 6

PREP TIME: 10 minutes, plus 2 hours chilling time

COOK TIME: 8 minutes

MAKE-AHEAD: The sabayon can be made up to 1 day ahead and kept refrigerated.

¾ cup heavy cream

2½ ounces good-quality bittersweet chocolate (60% cacao), finely chopped

⅓ cup plus 1 teaspoon sugar

½ cup dry Marsala wine

8 large egg yolks

Pinch of salt

2 tablespoons crème fraîche

2 cups fresh raspberries

A classic sabayon is an ultrarich French dessert or sauce that's made by whisking eggs, sugar, and sweet wine over simmering water until it's thick and creamy. I add chocolate to my sabayon because that's just what we chocoholics do. You could serve it warm, straight off the stove, and pour it into bowls or drizzle over berries, but I prefer to chill it so it has a thicker, mousse-like consistency.

1. In a small heavy saucepan, bring ¼ cup of the heavy cream just to a simmer over medium-high heat. Remove from the heat, add the chocolate, and stir just until melted and smooth. Set aside, covered to keep warm.

2. In a large heatproof bowl, whisk ⅓ cup of the sugar with the Marsala, egg yolks, and salt to blend. Set the bowl over a saucepan of simmering water (do not allow the bottom of the bowl to touch the water) and, using a large flexible whisk, beat the egg mixture for about 8 minutes, or until thick and creamy; an instant-read thermometer inserted into the mixture should register 140°F.

3. Using a large silicone spatula, fold about ¼ cup of the sabayon into the warm chocolate mixture to lighten it, then fold the lightened chocolate mixture into the remaining sabayon. Cover and refrigerate for about 2 hours, or until cold. (If desired, the sabayon can be divided among dessert bowls before it is refrigerated.)

4. When ready to serve, in a large bowl, whisk the remaining ½ cup heavy cream and the crème fraîche with the remaining 1 teaspoon sugar until thick and fluffy.

5. Spoon the sabayon onto plates or into small bowls (if you didn't chill the sabayon in bowls). Spoon a dollop of the whipped cream alongside or on top of each serving, scatter the raspberries over, and serve.

Passion Fruit Curd with Grilled Peaches and Apricots

I grew up eating loads of passion fruit; they're a real national treasure in Australia. I used to cut them in half and suck the bittersweet pulp right out of its skin for an after-school snack, not giving a hoot about the juices running down my face and onto my clothes (sorry, Mum). Now that I've put down roots in America, I've planted passion fruit trees in my backyard for a daily reminder of and connection to my home. One of the vines has crept all over the side of the house, which could be a pain, but I adore its wild roaming nature just as much as the fruit that it bears. Enjoy this luscious curd spooned over grilled stone fruits in the summertime, or spread it over thick-sliced toast.

SERVES: 4

PREP TIME: 5 minutes, plus 1 hour cooling time

COOK TIME: 5 minutes

MAKE-AHEAD: The curd will keep for up to 5 days, covered and refrigerated.

CURD

4 passion fruits

6 tablespoons sugar

1 large egg

1 large egg yolk

4 tablespoons (½ stick) unsalted butter, cut into small dice

6 firm but ripe peaches, halved and pitted

4 firm but ripe apricots, halved and pitted

Sugar, for dredging

1. To make the curd, cut the passion fruits in half and scoop their pulp, juice, and seeds into a medium heatproof bowl (you should have ⅓ cup). Whisk in the sugar, egg, and egg yolk to blend. Set the bowl over a saucepan of simmering water (do not allow the bottom of the bowl to touch the water) and whisk constantly for about 4 minutes, or until the mixture thickens. Remove from the heat and gradually whisk in the butter. Refrigerate for about 1 hour, or until cold.

2. To grill the fruit, prepare a grill for high heat.

3. Dredge the cut side of the peaches and apricots in sugar and shake off any excess sugar. Lightly oil the grill grates, add the peaches and apricots cut side down, cover with the lid, and grill for about 3 minutes, or until grill marks have formed on the fruit and the flesh has softened.

4. Transfer the peaches and apricots to a serving platter or four individual plates. Spoon about 1 tablespoon of the curd over each peach and apricot half and serve immediately.

Pavlova with Strawberries and Rhubarb

Good ol' Aussie Pav . . . or is it good ol' New Zealand Pav?! This dessert was created to honor Anna Pavlova, the amazing Russian ballerina, who first toured Australia *and* New Zealand in 1926. There is debate to this day over which country invented it (ahem, Australia, of course). Whatever the case, this billowy meringue with its marshmallowy center and crisp, delicate crust is a must-make for your next grilling gig. Celebrate the season by topping the Pav with strawberries and deep red rhubarb, or your choice of seasonal fruits, or for an alternative topping, spoon on cream and finish with the Passion Fruit Curd (see page 155).

1. To make the meringue, position a rack in the lower third of the oven and preheat the oven to 300°F. Line a large baking sheet with parchment paper and draw an 8-inch circle on the parchment.

2. In the bowl of a stand mixer fitted with the whisk attachment, beat the egg whites until foamy. Gradually add the sugar, beating on medium-high speed for about 10 minutes, or until firm glossy peaks form. Beat in the vinegar, vanilla, and salt. Sift the cornstarch over the meringue and gently fold it in.

3. Using a large spoon, dollop the meringue into the center of the circle on the prepared baking sheet. Spread the meringue decoratively, keeping it within the circle (the meringue will expand slightly as it bakes).

4. Place the Pavlova in the oven, immediately reduce the oven temperature to 225°F, and bake for about 1 hour, or until the meringue is crisp on the outside but still has a marshmallow-like center and puffs ever so slightly. Turn off the oven, prop the oven door open with a wooden spoon, and leave the meringue in the oven for 30 minutes, then remove from the oven and cool completely.

5. To prepare the fruit, in a medium heavy saucepan, whisk the amaretto and honey over medium-high heat until the mixture simmers. Add the rhubarb and return the mixture to a simmer, then immediately remove the pan from the heat. Set aside for about 5 minutes, or until the rhubarb softens slightly but does not become mushy.

(continued)

SERVES: 6 to 8

PREP TIME: 30 minutes, plus 1 hour cooling time

COOK TIME: 1½ hours

MAKE-AHEAD: The meringue can be made up to 8 hours ahead, cooled, covered, and stored at room temperature.

MERINGUE

6 large egg whites

1¾ cups superfine sugar

1 teaspoon distilled white vinegar

½ teaspoon pure vanilla extract

¼ teaspoon kosher salt

2 tablespoons plus 2 teaspoons cornstarch

TOPPING

3 tablespoons amaretto or other almond-flavored liqueur

3 tablespoons honey (preferably lavender honey)

6 ounces fresh rhubarb, thinly sliced diagonally

8 ounces small fresh strawberries, hulled and halved

1½ cups heavy cream

1 teaspoon pure almond extract

2 tablespoons finely chopped toasted pistachios

Powdered sugar, for sifting

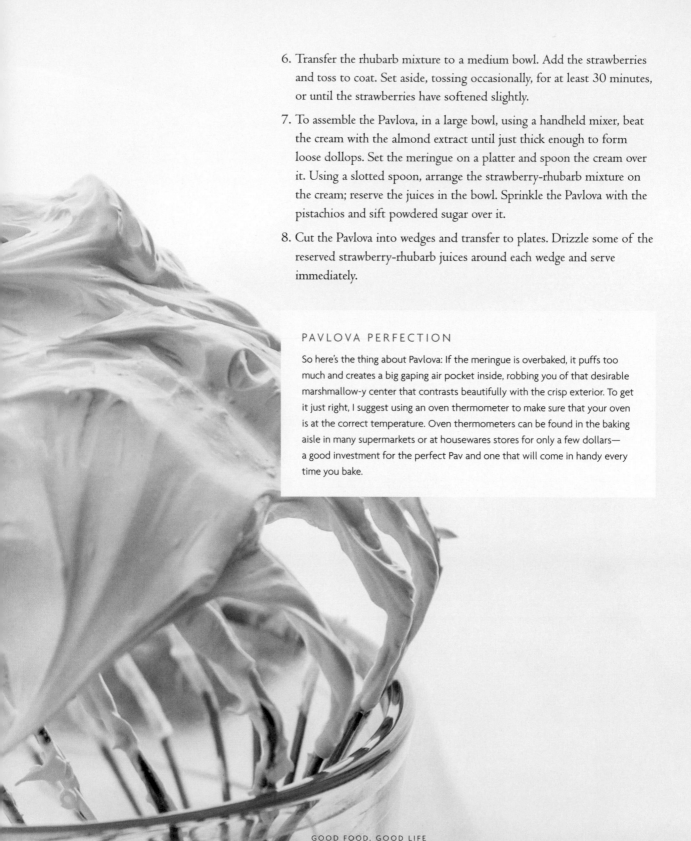

6. Transfer the rhubarb mixture to a medium bowl. Add the strawberries and toss to coat. Set aside, tossing occasionally, for at least 30 minutes, or until the strawberries have softened slightly.

7. To assemble the Pavlova, in a large bowl, using a handheld mixer, beat the cream with the almond extract until just thick enough to form loose dollops. Set the meringue on a platter and spoon the cream over it. Using a slotted spoon, arrange the strawberry-rhubarb mixture on the cream; reserve the juices in the bowl. Sprinkle the Pavlova with the pistachios and sift powdered sugar over it.

8. Cut the Pavlova into wedges and transfer to plates. Drizzle some of the reserved strawberry-rhubarb juices around each wedge and serve immediately.

PAVLOVA PERFECTION

So here's the thing about Pavlova: If the meringue is overbaked, it puffs too much and creates a big gaping air pocket inside, robbing you of that desirable marshmallow-y center that contrasts beautifully with the crisp exterior. To get it just right, I suggest using an oven thermometer to make sure that your oven is at the correct temperature. Oven thermometers can be found in the baking aisle in many supermarkets or at housewares stores for only a few dollars— a good investment for the perfect Pav and one that will come in handy every time you bake.

Roasted Banana Soufflés with Caramel Sauce

A silence fell over the table when my friends first tasted this dessert, interrupted only by the sound of spoons being licked or dipped back into the ramekins for a second, then third mouthful. A silencing dessert is always a winning dessert in my book.

SERVES: 4

PREP TIME: 15 minutes, plus 30 minutes cooling time

COOK TIME: 50 minutes

MAKE-AHEAD: The banana custard can be made up to 1 day ahead, covered and refrigerated. Bring to room temperature before proceeding.

1. Position a rack in the center of the oven, place a heavy baking sheet on the rack, and preheat the oven to 375°F. Completely coat the interiors of four 8-ounce ramekins (3½-inch diameter) with some of the butter, with your brush strokes going from the bottom of the ramekins to the top (this will help the soufflés rise better). Refrigerate for about 2 minutes, or until the butter is cold and set. Brush with a second coating of butter in the same manner. Then coat the interiors with sugar and shake out any excess sugar. Refrigerate the ramekins.

2. Place the bananas on a baking sheet lined with foil and roast for about 30 minutes, or until the banana peels are completely blackened and the flesh is soft. Remove the bananas from the oven (leave the oven on).

3. Peel the bananas (you should have about 1 heaping cup of banana flesh). Transfer to a blender, add the cream and milk, and puree until smooth.

4. Transfer the banana mixture to a medium heavy saucepan. Scrape the seeds from the vanilla bean into the mixture and bring to a simmer over medium heat.

5. Meanwhile, in a medium bowl, whisk 2 tablespoons of the granulated sugar and the yolks for about 1 minute, or until light and fluffy. Whisk in the flour, then whisk in the hot banana mixture. Return the mixture to the saucepan and cook, stirring constantly, over medium-high heat for about 2 minutes, or until the custard is very thick and just beginning to bubble. Transfer the custard to a large bowl, press a sheet of plastic wrap directly on the surface of the custard to prevent a skin from forming, and cool for 30 minutes, or to room temperature.

Unsalted butter, for the ramekins, at room temperature

6 tablespoons granulated sugar, plus more for the ramekins

2 large ripe bananas, unpeeled

⅔ cup heavy cream, at room temperature

⅔ cup whole milk, at room temperature

½ vanilla bean, split lengthwise

3 large eggs, separated

1½ tablespoons all-purpose flour

2 large egg whites

Powdered sugar, for dusting

¾ cup Caramel Sauce (recipe follows)

(continued)

6. In the bowl of a stand mixer fitted with the whisk attachment, whisk the egg whites on medium-high speed for about 1 minute, or until they begin to foam. Slowly rain in the remaining 4 tablespoons granulated sugar and beat for about 3 minutes, or until peaks are nearly stiff and still moist. Alternatively, you can use a handheld mixer instead of a stand mixer, but mixing times will be a bit longer.

7. Whisk one-third of the whipped egg whites into the banana custard to lighten it. Fold in another one-third of the egg whites, then fold in the remaining egg whites. Divide the mixture evenly among the prepared ramekins.

8. Bake the soufflés for about 15 minutes, or until they have risen but are still a bit liquid in the center. Dust with powdered sugar and serve immediately, with the caramel sauce.

FOR EASY WOW FACTOR

Dust the soufflés with powdered sugar at the table and serve the caramel sauce in a bowl with a couple of spoons so your guests can drizzle as much sauce over their dessert as they please. If your friends are anything like mine, there won't be a scrap of sauce left over for tomorrow night's ice cream.

Caramel Sauce

If you've got sugar, cream, butter, and salt on hand, you can pull caramel sauce out of your hat in a matter of minutes. The caramel sauce can be made up to 3 days ahead, covered, and refrigerated. Rewarm over low heat.

MAKES: 1½ cups

1⅔ cups sugar
⅔ cup heavy cream
½ cup (1 stick) unsalted butter, at room temperature
¾ teaspoon fleur de sel

1. Heat a medium heavy saucepan over medium heat. Add the sugar and cook, without stirring, for about 5 minutes, or until the sugar melts and then turns a deep amber color. As the sugar melts and caramelizes, tilt and swirl the pan to distribute the caramel evenly, but do not stir. As soon as the caramel is a deep amber color, remove the pan from the heat.

2. Stir in the cream and butter, whisking until the butter melts and the sauce is completely blended. Strain through a fine-mesh sieve to remove any undissolved bits of sugar, if necessary. Stir in the fleur de sel and cool slightly before serving.

Chilled Yellow Watermelon Soup with Summer Berries

I first made this elegant and refreshing soup for an episode of *Take Home Chef* that we filmed in Santa Fe and since then I haven't let a summer slip by without making it. The contrast of the vibrant berries against the pureed yellow watermelon (peak season: June to August) makes for a stunning-looking soup, but red watermelon will do just fine too.

1. In a blender, combine the watermelon, mint, and lime juice and blend until the mint is finely chopped. Strain the soup through a fine-mesh sieve into a medium bowl. Cover and refrigerate for about 2 hours, or until well chilled.

2. Mix all the berries together and then mound in the center of four wide soup bowls. Dust with powdered sugar. Carefully pour the chilled soup around the fruit and serve.

SERVES: 4

PREP TIME: 10 minutes, plus 2 hours chilling time

MAKE-AHEAD: The soup can be made up to 6 hours ahead and kept refrigerated.

1 small yellow watermelon (4 to 5 pounds), rind and any large seeds removed and flesh coarsely chopped

⅓ cup firmly packed fresh mint leaves

⅓ cup fresh lime juice

6 ounces fresh small strawberries (about 1 cup), hulled and halved, quartered if large

4 ounces fresh blueberries (about 1 cup)

4 ounces fresh raspberries (about 1 cup)

2 ounces fresh blackberries (about ½ cup)

Powdered sugar, for dusting

Ricotta Fritters with Quick Mixed Berry Jam

MAKES: about 20 fritters

PREP TIME: 5 minutes

COOK TIME: 12 minutes

MAKE-AHEAD: The fritter batter can be made up to 2 hours ahead, covered and refrigerated.

Canola oil, for deep-frying

1 cup all-purpose flour

¼ cup powdered sugar, plus more for dusting

2 teaspoons baking powder

¼ teaspoon salt

1 cup Homemade Ricotta (page 106) or good-quality fresh whole-milk ricotta

2 large eggs, beaten to blend

½ cup whole milk

2 teaspoons grated orange zest

Quick Mixed Berry Jam (recipe follows)

My friends go absolutely gaga when I make these, crispy on the outside and tender on the inside, at home. What better way is there to end a meal than piping hot fritters (read: doughnuts) with a fresh berry filling? Happy food, happy life. The warmth of these bad boys extends to those at the table.

1. Pour 3 inches of oil into a large wide heavy saucepan and heat over medium-high heat until it reaches 350°F.

2. Meanwhile, in a medium bowl, whisk the flour, powdered sugar, baking powder, and salt to blend. In a large bowl, whisk the ricotta, eggs, milk, and orange zest to blend, then whisk in the flour mixture.

3. Working in batches, fill a 1¼-ounce ice cream scoop with batter, lower the scoop into the hot oil, and release the batter while the scoop is submerged in the oil, to achieve a circular shape; repeat to make more fritters, without crowding the pan. Fry the fritters, turning occasionally, for 3 to 4 minutes, or until they are deep golden brown and cooked through. Using a slotted spoon, transfer the fritters to paper towels to drain. Return the oil to 350°F between batches.

4. Dust the warm fritters with powdered sugar and serve with the jam alongside, or fill the fritters with the jam (see Note).

FRITTERS FOUR WAYS

- Make "churros" by rolling fritters in cinnamon sugar (½ cup granulated sugar to 2 teaspoons ground cinnamon) instead of dusting them with powdered sugar, and serve with warm bittersweet chocolate sabayon (see page 154).
- Dust the fritters with Chamomile Sugar (page 168) and serve with Caramel Sauce (page 160).
- Split the fritters and spoon passion fruit curd (see page 155) into the centers.
- Make jam-filled fritters: Strain the jam through a fine-mesh sieve and discard the solids. Fill a flavor injector with the strained jam. Insert the flavor injector needle into the center of each fritter and pipe the jam into the fritter. Dust the fritters with powdered sugar and serve.

Quick Mixed Berry Jam

This summer jam will keep for up to 1 week, stored airtight in the refrigerator.

MAKES: about 2 cups

¾ cup fresh raspberries
⅔ cup fresh blueberries
½ cup fresh blackberries
¾ cup sugar
2 tablespoons fresh lemon juice

1. In a medium heavy skillet, combine the berries, sugar, and lemon juice and bring the mixture to a simmer over medium heat, mashing the berries with a fork. Simmer the mixture, stirring frequently, for about 5 minutes, or until it thickens slightly, into a very loose jam consistency.

2. Remove the pan from the heat and set the jam aside to cool to room temperature for about 20 minutes, stirring occasionally.

Magic Caramel Bars

The original Magic Bars, also called 7-Layer Bars, surfaced in the '60s and people have been putting their own spin on these dangerously delicious treats ever since. This is an elevated version: it has a shortbread crust, slight bitterness from the espresso powder, sweetness from the coconut milk–infused caramel, and awesome crunch from the top layer of rich, buttery macadamias. Scrumptious to eat while sipping on a French Press Coffee (page 269).

1. To make the crust, preheat the oven 350°F. Spray a 9 x 9 x 2-inch baking pan with nonstick cooking spray.

2. In a food processor, pulse the flour, powdered sugar, and salt until blended. Add the butter and pulse 5 or 6 times, until the mixture resembles coarse bread crumbs. Add 3 tablespoons ice water and process until moist clumps of dough form, adding more ice water by the teaspoonful if the dough seems dry.

3. Transfer the crust mixture to the prepared pan and press it evenly over the bottom of the pan. Using a fork, poke holes halfway through the crust. Bake for about 30 minutes, or until the crust is light golden and the edges are beginning to pull away from the sides of the pan. Set aside to cool for 5 minutes. (Leave the oven on.)

4. Meanwhile, to make the caramel, in a medium heavy saucepan, combine the coconut milk, brown sugar, and honey and bring to a boil over medium-high heat, stirring until the sugar dissolves. Continue to boil for about 7 minutes, or until the mixture darkens and has reduced by half. You should have 1 cup of caramel. Set aside.

5. To assemble the bars, sprinkle the chocolate chips over the baked crust, then sprinkle the espresso powder over the chocolate. Top with a layer of the macadamia nuts. Drizzle the caramel evenly over the top.

6. Bake for about 15 minutes, or until the topping is golden brown and bubbling thickly. Loosen the bars from the sides of the pan while still warm and cool completely in the pan on a wire rack, then refrigerate for about 1 hour, or until cold.

7. Using a small sharp knife, loosen the edges from the sides of the baking pan. Using two spatulas, carefully remove the bars from the pan and transfer to a cutting board. Trim off the sticky edges (about ¼ inch). Cut into eighteen 2½ x 1-inch rectangles.

MAKES: 18 bars

PREP TIME: 20 minutes, plus 1 hour cooling time

COOK TIME: 45 minutes

MAKE-AHEAD: The bars will keep for up to 2 days, cooled completely and stored airtight at room temperature.

CRUST

Nonstick vegetable oil cooking spray

1¾ cups all-purpose flour

⅓ cup powdered sugar

1 teaspoon salt

10 tablespoons (1¼ sticks) chilled unsalted butter, cut into ½-inch cubes

About 3 tablespoons ice water

TOPPING

1 cup unsweetened coconut milk

¼ cup packed light brown sugar

¼ cup honey

2 cups (about 12 ounces) semisweet chocolate chips

1½ teaspoons espresso powder

1 cup coarsely chopped toasted macadamia nuts

Pizzelle with Chamomile Sugar

MAKES: about 24 pizzelle

PREP TIME: 5 minutes, plus 1 hour for the batter to rest

COOK TIME: 15 minutes

MAKE-AHEAD: The pizzelle will keep for up to 5 days, stored in an airtight container at room temperature.

PIZZELLE

½ cup granulated sugar

1 large egg

1½ tablespoons canola oil

1 tablespoon water

2 teaspoons pure vanilla extract

¼ teaspoon salt

½ cup plus 1 tablespoon all-purpose flour

About 2 tablespoons (¼ stick) unsalted butter, at room temperature

CHAMOMILE SUGAR

2 tablespoons powdered sugar

1 tablespoon chamomile tea

Pizzelle are Italian wafer cookies cooked in a pizzelle iron with snowflake-like molds. You can buy pizzelle in packets from some gourmet food stores, but these are the most delicate and dainty pizzelle that I've ever eaten. Making them is similar to and as simple as making breakfast waffles. Dunk a pizzella into the Weeknight Belgian Hot Chocolate (page 266) for a naughty nightcap treat.

1. In a large bowl, whisk the sugar, egg, oil, water, vanilla, and salt to blend. Add the flour and whisk just until blended. Cover and refrigerate for 1 hour.

2. Meanwhile, to make the chamomile sugar, in a clean coffee grinder or spice mill, grind the powdered sugar and chamomile to a powder. Set aside.

3. Preheat an electric pizzelle iron (with three 3-inch-diameter grids) to medium-high heat. Lightly brush the cooking surfaces with some of the butter. Spoon 1 to 1½ teaspoons of batter into the center of each grid, close the iron, and cook for about 1 minute, or until most of the steam rising from the iron has dissipated and the pizzelle are golden. (You may need to adjust the heat level and cooking time, as pizzelle irons vary.) The pizzelle will be very thin and delicate and will become crisp as they cool. Transfer the pizzelle to a cooling rack and cool completely. Repeat with the remaining batter.

4. Sift the chamomile sugar over the cooled pizzelle.

Fresh Mint Chip Gelato

MAKES: about 1 quart

PREP TIME: 10 minutes, plus 7½ hours cooling and freezing time

COOK TIME: 10 minutes

MAKE-AHEAD: The gelato can be made up to 5 days ahead.

1 cup sugar

2 tablespoons cornstarch

2 cups heavy cream

2 cups whole milk

6 fresh mint sprigs

4 ounces bittersweet chocolate (70% cacao), chopped

Mint and chocolate were made for each other and, when combined, just happen to be my favorite gelato flavor. Top with some whipped crème fraîche, or for an out-of-this-world ice cream sandwich (see photograph on page 140) carrying a real fresh mint flavor, gently press a scoop of the freshly churned gelato between two pizzelle (see page 168) and enjoy immediately.

1. In a large heavy saucepan, stir the sugar and cornstarch to blend. Whisk in the cream and milk and cook over medium heat, whisking constantly, for about 10 minutes, or until the mixture thickens and begins to bubble.

2. Transfer the cream mixture to a heatproof bowl and add the mint. Set the bowl over a bowl of ice water to cool the mixture down quickly and stir occasionally until cool; discard the mint after 5 minutes. Just don't steep the mint for too long or it will impart a grassy flavor; a quick steep while the cream cools will do. Cover the mint cream and refrigerate for about 4 hours, or until completely cold.

3. Freeze the mint cream in an ice cream maker according to the manufacturer's instructions until frozen.

4. Meanwhile, place the chocolate in a heatproof bowl, set it over a saucepan of simmering water, and stir the chocolate until it has just melted. Remove from the heat and cool until the chocolate is barely warm and still fluid.

5. Transfer the gelato to a large bowl set over a bowl of ice. Working quickly, drizzle the melted chocolate into the gelato while whisking or stirring vigorously. The chocolate will flake apart as it hits the cold gelato, forming bits of chocolate throughout. If you prefer larger pieces of chocolate throughout the gelato, use a wooden spoon to slowly stir in the melted chocolate. Serve immediately, or transfer to a container and freeze for 3 hours, or until firm.

GELATO STYLE

If you've been afraid of making ice cream, fear no more! This one is made gelato style, so it forgoes the potentially intimidating egg-based custard used in traditional ice cream. Instead, an eggless custard is thickened with cornstarch for the gelato base. So easy.

Lime Granita with Oranges

SERVES: 8

PREP TIME: 10 minutes, plus about 6 hours cooling, chilling, and freezing time

COOK TIME: 2 minutes

MAKE-AHEAD: The granita can be made up to 3 days ahead.

2½ cups water

1 cup sugar

2 tablespoons Lyle's Golden Syrup

2 teaspoons finely grated lime zest

¾ cup fresh lime juice (from about 5 limes)

1 orange (preferably Cara Cara), segmented, seeds removed, and cut into small cubes

I originally created this as a refreshing and zesty sorbet for my restaurant Maude's very first menu item back in February 2014. I'm crazy about my little L.A. restaurant, and what better way to honor it than to share its launching dish right here. If you have an ice cream machine, you can churn the lime mixture into sorbet instead (see Note). Lyle's Golden Syrup is a British product that is sweet and sticky, like corn syrup, but made purely from sugar. It is available at most supermarkets, but you can also order it online.

1. In a medium saucepan, combine the water and sugar and bring to a simmer over medium heat, stirring until the sugar has dissolved. Stir in the syrup and zest, remove from the heat, and set aside to cool completely.

2. Whisk the lime juice into the cooled mixture and refrigerate until cold.

3. Strain the lime mixture and pour into a shallow baking dish. Place in the freezer and freeze for about 30 minutes, or until ice crystals start to form. Using a fork, scrape the mixture to break up the ice crystals. Freeze, scraping and breaking up the mixture every 30 minutes, for about 3 hours, or until the mixture resembles fluffy shaved ice.

4. Arrange a few orange cubes on each of eight small serving plates or bowls. Top with the granita and serve immediately.

LIME SORBET

Make, chill, and strain the lime mixture, then freeze in an ice cream maker according to the manufacturer's instructions. Transfer to a container, cover, and freeze for at least 3 hours, or until firm, before serving. Makes about 3 cups.

Chapter 5

IN THE MORNING

———

Brekky. I have a love/hate relationship with what we Aussies call breakfast. I know how unbelievably good it can be, but sometimes I just don't have time for it. When I have a super early start, I literally run through the kitchen, thinking, "Gosh, do I have my coffee now or at the restaurant?" That's why I've pulled together some incredible recipes that can be made ahead and kept in the fridge for up to three days. So, if you make Yogurt Parfaits with Blackberries and Vanilla or Golden Granola with Home-made Almond Milk on the weekend, you've always got a delicious fallback. I know that eating Bircher muesli on my lap when I'm sitting at a red light isn't a perfect start to the day, but it tastes awesome and it's nutritious—and sure beats skipping brekky altogether. After a bowl of this good stuff, I'm ready to meet the day head-on.

On those slower, quieter mornings—the best type of mornings—we let breakfast carry on until noon at our place. If friends are stopping by, it gives me the perfect excuse to flip crepes and smother them in a Maple-Kumquat Syrup or fry up all the leftover cured meats in my fridge for the ultimate melted cheese and sunny-side-up egg Brekky Bagel Sandwich.

Mornings have become extra-special to me now that I get to share them with my three-year-old son/sous chef, Hudson, who has mastered the art of whisking, stirring, and dishing out orders from his favorite work station: our kitchen sink. Hud and I brew some coffee, juice fruit and veggies from the garden, scramble eggs with spinach, and mix up muffin and crumpet batters. When he dips his little fingers in the muffin batter and says, with a nod of approval, "Yep, it's good, Dada," or asks me for the "honey honey" to spread over a crumpet, there's no better start to my day.

Morning Toast with Melted Raspberries

This amped-up version of toast with jam features fresh berries that are soft and syrupy but don't lose their shape or texture once "melted." The buttery toast makes a great match because the bread soaks up all of the juices, but I can think of plenty of other good homes for the melted berries—on top of Pavlova, waffles or pancakes, yogurt, granola, vanilla ice cream, in cocktails . . . the list is endless.

SERVES: 4

PREP TIME: 10 minutes

COOK TIME: 3 minutes

MAKE-AHEAD: The toast and berries should be served as soon as they are made.

3 tablespoons salted butter, at room temperature

8 ½-inch-thick slices of your favorite bread

12 ounces fresh raspberries

¼ cup pure maple syrup

2 teaspoons finely grated lemon zest

1. Preheat the broiler (you can use a toaster oven). Spread the butter over one side of each slice of bread. Arrange the bread on a small baking sheet and broil for 3 to 4 minutes, or until the tops are golden brown and crisp.

2. Meanwhile, heat a large heavy skillet over medium-high heat. Add the raspberries, maple syrup, and zest and cook for about 1 minute, or until the berries soften just slightly and begin to release enough juice to form a syrup. Don't let the berries cook too long, or they will become mushy and lose their beautiful shape.

3. Spoon the warm berry mixture over the toast and serve immediately.

SEASONAL EATING

I'm sure you've noticed that the price of a half-pint of raspberries can be jacked up to around $6 in their off-season, and their flavor is dull and watery as well, so be sure to buy berries in the summertime. They'll be much cheaper and will explode with flavor.

Sunday Berry-Almond Pastries

SERVES: 8

PREP TIME: 10 minutes

COOK TIME: 18 minutes

MAKE-AHEAD: The pastries will keep for up to 2 days, stored airtight at room temperature.

All-purpose flour, for dusting

1 17.3-ounce package frozen puff pastry (2 sheets), thawed

1 7-ounce package almond paste

3 cups assorted fresh berries (about 1 pound)

1 large egg, beaten to blend

½ cup powdered sugar

2 tablespoons (¼ stick) unsalted butter, melted

1 tablespoon water

Most people are accustomed to eating store-bought pastries, so it's always a special treat when you pull out a batch of the freshly baked homemade kind. Kids have a ball making them too. Hudson loves to drop the berries onto the squares and seal the triangles with his little fingers. The pastries ooze with warm syrupy berries, and the crumbly almond paste becomes smooth and creamy when baked. In fact, these are too good to eat only on Sundays.

1. Preheat the oven to 400°F. Line a baking sheet with parchment paper.

2. One at a time, on a lightly floured work surface, roll out each sheet of pastry to an 11-inch square and cut into 4 squares (for a total of 8 squares). Turn a pastry square so one corner is toward you and crumble one-eighth of the almond paste over the bottom half of the square, leaving a ¼-inch border along both edges. Top with one-eighth of the mixed berries and fold the top half of the pastry square over the filling to form a triangle. Press the edges together, crimp with a fork to seal, and transfer to the prepared baking sheet. Repeat with the remaining squares and fillings.

3. Using a pastry brush, brush the tops of the pastries with the beaten egg. Cut 3 slits in the top of each one. Bake for about 18 minutes, or until the pastries are golden brown and the filling is starting to bubble. Remove from the oven.

4. In a small bowl, whisk the powdered sugar, butter, and water until smooth. Drizzle over the pastries and serve warm.

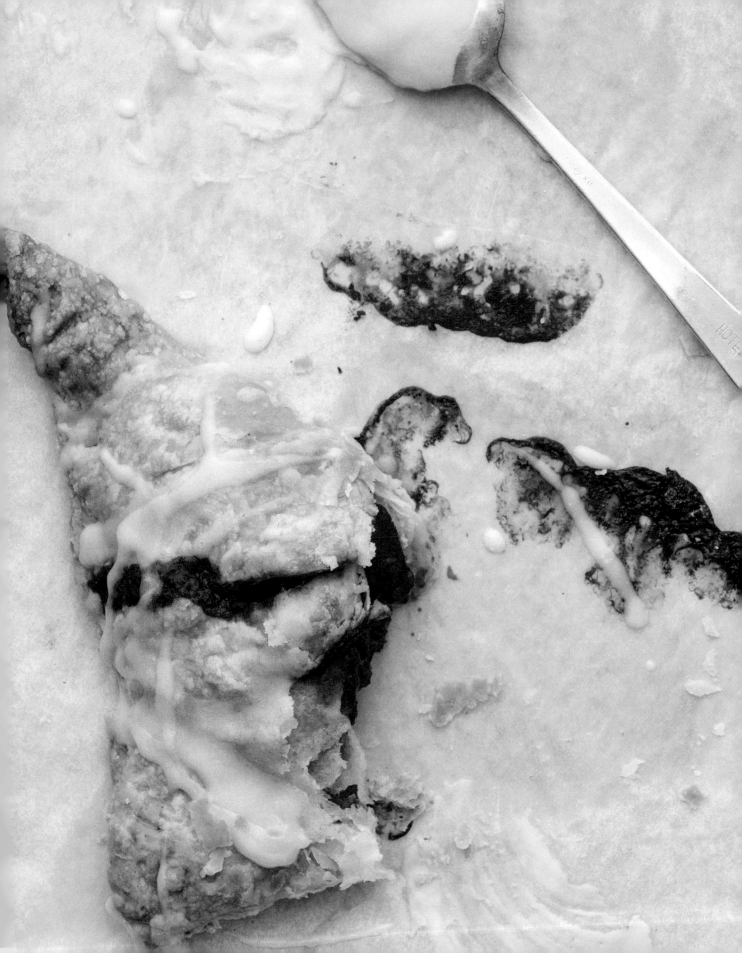

Bircher Muesli with Seasonal Toppings

Aussies have taken to eating Bircher muesli as if it was one of our own who created it, but we can't take the credit for this breakfast staple. Swiss physician Maximilian Bircher-Benner came up with it as a healthy, no-bake breakfast option packed with grated apple, oats, yogurt, and juice. The seasonal toppings are tasty suggestions but you can sub in whatever you like. Cheers, Max!

SERVES: 4 (makes 5 cups)

PREP TIME: 15 minutes, plus overnight refrigeration

COOK TIME: 10 minutes

MAKE-AHEAD: The muesli will keep for up to 3 days, covered, and refrigerated.

1. Using a box grater, coarsely grate the apples into a large bowl. Mix in the oats, yogurt, apple juice, and cinnamon. Cover and refrigerate overnight.

2. Divide the muesli among four bowls. Top with your chosen topping and serve.

2 Gala apples, quartered and cored (not peeled)

2 cups old-fashioned rolled oats

2 cups plain low-fat yogurt

1 cup apple juice

¼ teaspoon ground cinnamon

Topping of your choice (recipes follow)

Fall Topping: Poached Dried Apricots and Pistachios

1 cup dried apricots, halved
½ cup water
⅓ cup honey
⅓ cup shelled pistachios, toasted and chopped

1. In a small heavy saucepan, combine the dried apricots, water, and honey. Bring to a simmer over medium-low heat, and simmer gently for about 10 minutes, or until the apricots are plump and very tender and the syrup has thickened slightly. Cool completely.

2. To serve, spoon the apricot mixture over the muesli and sprinkle with the pistachios.

Winter Topping: Tangerines and Pecans

3 small tangerines
½ cup pure maple syrup
½ cup pecans, toasted and coarsely broken

1. Using a Microplane grater, finely grate 1 teaspoon tangerine zest into a small heavy saucepan. Add the maple syrup, bring to a simmer over medium-low heat, and simmer gently for about 5 minutes, or until the syrup thickens slightly. Cool completely.

2. To serve, drizzle the maple syrup over the muesli and sprinkle with the pecans. Peel and segment the tangerines and place a few tangerine segments on top of each bowl of muesli.

Summer Topping: Peaches and Coconut-Almond Crumble

½ cup unsweetened shredded coconut

½ cup sliced raw almonds

2 tablespoons sugar

1 egg white, stirred to blend

3 firm but ripe peaches, halved, pitted, and cut into ½-inch wedges

1. Preheat the oven to 300°F. Line a baking sheet with parchment paper.

2. In a medium bowl, toss the coconut, almonds, and sugar together. Stir in 2 tablespoons of the egg white, blending well. Spread the mixture on the prepared baking sheet and bake for about 15 minutes, or until the crumble is crisp and golden brown. Cool completely.

3. To serve, top the muesli with the peaches and sprinkle the crumble over the top.

Spring Topping: Rhubarb and Hazelnuts

4 slender rhubarb stalks (about 10 ounces total), cut into ½-inch slices

⅓ cup sugar

1 tablespoon fresh lemon juice

½ cup hazelnuts, toasted, skinned, and coarsely chopped

1. In a medium heavy skillet, combine the rhubarb, sugar, and lemon juice and bring to a simmer over medium-high heat, stirring to dissolve the sugar, then continue to cook, stirring often, for about 3 minutes, or until the juices have thickened slightly and the rhubarb is tender but not falling apart. Cool completely.

2. To serve, spoon the rhubarb mixture over the muesli and top with the hazelnuts.

Walnut-Date Muffins

MAKES: 12 muffins

PREP TIME: 15 minutes

COOK TIME: 22 minutes

MAKE-AHEAD: The muffins can be made up to 2 days ahead and stored airtight at room temperature.

1½ cups old-fashioned rolled oats

1 cup unbleached all-purpose flour

2 teaspoons baking powder

½ teaspoon baking soda

10 tablespoons (1¼ sticks) unsalted butter, at room temperature

¼ cup packed light brown sugar

3 tablespoons honey

1 tablespoon finely grated orange zest

½ teaspoon salt

½ teaspoon ground cinnamon

2 large eggs

⅔ cup plain low-fat yogurt

1½ cups walnuts, toasted and coarsely chopped

12 dates, pitted and chopped

For this healthier alternative to the typical sugar-and-fat-filled muffins, oats are combined with walnuts and dates and just a touch of brown sugar and honey. Yogurt replaces some of the butter, while dates and honey replace most of the sugar. They're perfect fresh outta the oven or for the next day's morning rush.

1. Preheat the oven to 375°F. Line a muffin pan with paper muffin liners.

2. In a medium bowl, mix the oats, flour, baking powder, and baking soda to blend.

3. In a large bowl, using a handheld mixer, beat the butter, brown sugar, honey, orange zest, salt, and cinnamon until creamy. Beat in the eggs one at a time, beating well after each addition, then beat in the yogurt. Add the oat mixture and stir just until blended. Using a silicone spatula, fold in the walnuts and dates.

4. Divide the batter equally among the muffin cups. Bake for 20 to 22 minutes, or until the muffins are golden and a toothpick inserted into the center of one comes out with just a few moist crumbs attached. Cool the muffins slightly on a rack and serve warm, or let cool to room temperature.

Golden Granola with Homemade Almond Milk

I feel awesome when I take a little time out on a Sunday afternoon to whip up a batch of granola and almond milk for the week ahead. Then I'm never left scratching my head over what to have for breakfast during the week, because my homemade cereal is waiting for me—I just need to add a dash of milk and/or yogurt and fruit to be feeling full of good stuff until lunch. The chewy dried cherries and figs are winning ingredients in the crunchy granola, but other dried fruits will be delicious too. Double or triple the recipe if you've got a big hungry family; it'll keep in an airtight container for a week. Granola is also a great snack on its own. Just throw a handful into a sealable plastic bag, take to school or work, and eat straight from the bag. It's a nice, sweet boost for that 3 p.m. slump.

SERVES: 4 (Makes about 4 cups)

PREP TIME: 10 minutes

COOK TIME: 20 minutes

MAKE-AHEAD: The granola can be made up to 1 week ahead and stored airtight at room temperature.

2 cups old-fashioned rolled oats
1 cup chopped raw whole almonds
3 tablespoons ground flaxseeds
⅔ cup honey
3 tablespoons canola oil
2 tablespoons grated tangerine zest
1 teaspoon pure almond extract
½ cup dried cherries
½ cup dried Calimyrna figs, diced
¼ cup golden raisins
About 3 cups Homemade Almond Milk (page 265)

1. Preheat the oven to 350°F. Lightly oil a large heavy baking sheet.

2. In a large bowl, toss the oats, almonds, and ground flaxseeds to blend.

3. In a small heavy saucepan, combine the honey, oil, and tangerine zest and bring to a simmer over medium heat. Remove from the heat and stir in the almond extract. Stir the honey mixture into the oat mixture and spread on the prepared baking sheet.

4. Bake, stirring occasionally, for about 15 minutes, or until the granola is pale golden brown. Stir in the dried cherries, figs, and raisins and bake for about 5 minutes longer, or until the granola is a rich golden brown. Cool completely (the granola will crisp as it cools).

5. Divide the granola among four bowls, pour the almond milk over, and serve.

Crêpes with Homemade Ricotta and Maple-Kumquat Syrup

These crêpes might not turn up on the breakfast table every morning, but when they do, it means we're in for a great day. With its unique sweet, sour, and slightly bitter flavor, the Maple-Kumquat Syrup is a showstopper, and it tastes especially good when balanced with mild homemade ricotta and tangy sour cream.

SERVES: 6

PREP TIME: 15 minutes, plus 30 minutes for the batter to rest

COOK TIME: 30 minutes

MAKE-AHEAD: The crêpes can be made up to 1 day ahead, covered, and refrigerated.

1. To make the crêpes, in a blender, combine the flour, milk, cream, eggs, sugar, and salt and blend until smooth. Cover and refrigerate for 30 minutes.

2. Heat a crêpe pan or heavy 8-inch nonstick skillet over medium-low heat. Dab some butter on a paper towel and wipe the pan with the butter. Pour 3 tablespoons of batter into the center of the pan and swirl to coat the bottom evenly. Cook for 1½ minutes, or until the edges of the crêpe are light brown. Using a silicone spatula, gently loosen the edges and carefully turn the crêpe over. Continue cooking for about 1 minute, or until the bottom begins to brown in spots. Transfer the crêpe to a plate. Repeat with the remaining batter, wiping the pan with butter as needed, until you have 12 crêpes.

3. To serve, preheat the oven to 350°F. Line a baking sheet with parchment paper.

4. In a large bowl, whisk the ricotta, egg, sugar, and salt to blend. Working with one crêpe at a time, spread about 2½ tablespoons of the ricotta filling over each crêpe, leaving a border around the edge, and fold it in half and then in half again, forming a triangle. Arrange the crêpes on the prepared baking sheet and bake for about 6 minutes, or until they are puffed and the filling is hot.

5. Place 2 crêpes on each of six plates. Spoon the warm maple-kumquat syrup over, spoon a dollop of sour cream on top of each crêpe, and serve.

CRÊPES

1 cup all-purpose flour, sifted

1¼ cups whole milk

½ cup heavy cream

2 large eggs

4 teaspoons sugar

Pinch of salt

About 1 tablespoon unsalted butter, at room temperature

FILLING

1½ cups Homemade Ricotta (page 106) or good-quality fresh whole-milk ricotta

1 large egg

2 tablespoons sugar

¼ teaspoon kosher salt

Maple-Kumquat Syrup (recipe follows), warm

1 cup sour cream

Maple-Kumquat Syrup

You can serve this winter syrup over a whole bunch of brekkys, such as French toast, pancakes, waffles, and crumpets, or use it to take desserts to new heights. Pour it over vanilla ice cream and top with crushed toasted pecans. Or put a kumquat spin on my rum pound cake (see page 150) by replacing the lime glaze with the syrup—brush enough to coat the cake and serve any leftover syrup alongside it. The syrup will keep for up to 3 days stored airtight in the refrigerator. Rewarm over low heat before serving.

MAKES: 2 cups

1½ cups pure maple syrup
3 cardamom pods, cracked open
1½ cups sliced kumquats (about 20 kumquats), seeds removed

In a small saucepan, combine the maple syrup and cardamom, bring to a simmer over medium heat, and simmer for 2 minutes. Remove the pan from the heat, stir in the kumquats, and let steep for 10 minutes. Discard the cardamom. Serve warm.

Smoked Salmon Omelet with Goat Cheese and Beet Relish

SERVES: 4

PREP TIME: 15 minutes

COOK TIME: 10 minutes

MAKE-AHEAD: The beet relish can be made up to 3 days ahead, covered, and refrigerated.

1 medium red beet, peeled

1½ tablespoons balsamic vinegar

1 tablespoon olive oil

1 tablespoon plus 2 teaspoons finely chopped fresh chives

1 tablespoon finely chopped fresh dill

½ teaspoon sugar

Kosher salt and freshly ground black pepper

8 large eggs

¼ cup whole milk

2 tablespoons (¼ stick) unsalted butter

6 ounces smoked salmon

4 ounces fresh goat cheese

Omelets are quick to make, full of protein, and versatile. You can fill them with crispy bacon, veggies, cheeses, herbs, a dash of hot sauce.... However, if you want to get a little fancy, try smoked salmon and goat cheese. I made this for Lindsay on Mother's Day, and it sent me straight into her good books for days. You want your eggs to be soft and fluffy, not overcooked and rubbery, so keep your attention on the pan. The easy beet relish adds sharp flavor—try it on hot dogs, burgers, or sandwiches.

1. To make the beet relish, using a box grater, coarsely grate the beet into a medium bowl. Stir in the vinegar, oil, 2 teaspoons each of the chives and dill, and the sugar. Season the relish to taste with salt and pepper. Set aside.

2. To make the omelets, in a large bowl, whisk the eggs and milk to blend. Season with salt.

3. Heat a medium nonstick skillet over medium-low heat. Add ½ tablespoon of the butter and swirl to coat. Pour in one-fourth of the egg mixture, swirling the pan to coat the bottom evenly, and cook, lifting up the edges with a silicone spatula and allowing the uncooked eggs to run onto the pan, for about 2 minutes, or until most of the egg is set but the omelet is still runny on top. Lay one-fourth of the salmon over the omelet, top with dollops of one-fourth of the cheese, and scatter about 1½ tablespoons of the beet relish over the top. Fold the omelet and transfer it to a plate. If desired, you can keep the omelet warm in a 200°F oven while you make more omelets. Repeat to make 3 more omelets.

4. Sprinkle the omelets with the remaining chives and dill and serve with the remaining beet relish.

Poached Eggs with Bacon, Avocado, and Lime Mojo

My "how to poach eggs" webisode shared on YouTube is one of my most-watched cooking tips, so I'm sharing a recipe to make 'em really POP! The citrusy Cuban mojo sauce (pronounced "*mo*-ho"), a light and refreshing alternative to hollandaise, coats the eggs and avocado and is drizzled over the dish right before serving to drive that flavor home. Serve with Spicy and Smoky Bloody Marys (page 262), and I'd say you're off to a bloody good start.

SERVES: 4

PREP TIME: 10 minutes

COOK TIME: 20 minutes

⅓ cup plus 1 tablespoon olive oil

2 limes

2 tablespoons chopped fresh cilantro, plus 12 whole leaves for garnish

1 scallion, trimmed and finely chopped

1 Fresno chile, finely chopped

2 tablespoons distilled white vinegar

4 large eggs

1 avocado, halved, pitted, peeled, and cut into large chunks

Kosher salt

4 ½-inch-thick slices ciabatta bread

2 tablespoons (¼ stick) salted butter

4 slices bacon, cooked and kept warm

Freshly ground black pepper

1. To make the lime mojo, in a small saucepan, heat ⅓ cup of the oil over medium-low heat until it reaches the temperature of a warm bath, about 100°F.

2. Meanwhile, using a Microplane grater, finely grate the zest of the limes into a medium bowl. Halve the limes and squeeze ¼ cup juice into the bowl. Stir in the chopped cilantro, scallion, and chile.

3. Add all but 1 tablespoon of the lime-herb mixture to the warm oil and remove the pan from the heat. Set aside.

4. To poach the eggs, in a large deep saucepan, combine the vinegar and 8 cups water and bring to a boil over high heat. Reduce the heat so that the water is just simmering. Crack 1 egg into a coffee cup or small bowl and gently transfer the egg to the simmering water. Repeat with the remaining eggs, spacing them evenly in the pan, and poach for about 3 minutes, or until the whites are set but the yolks are still fluid. Using a slotted spoon, carefully remove the eggs from the simmering water and place them in the warm olive oil–lime sauce; set aside.

5. Meanwhile, preheat the broiler (you can use a toaster oven). Gently fold the avocado chunks into the reserved lime-herb mixture to coat. Season with salt.

6. Spread the slices of ciabatta with the butter and broil for about 3 minutes, or until nicely toasted on top.

7. To serve, place the toast on four plates and top each piece with a slice of bacon. Divide the avocado among the toasts. Using a slotted spoon, carefully remove the eggs from the sauce and place them on top of the avocado. Season with salt and pepper. Drizzle about 1 tablespoon of sauce over each toast, distributing the herbs and chile evenly. Garnish with the cilantro leaves and serve immediately.

Maple Bran Madeleines

MAKES: 14 madeleines

PREP TIME: 10 minutes

COOK TIME: 20 minutes

MAKE-AHEAD: The madeleines are best
served warm, but they can be made up to
1 day ahead, cooled, and stored airtight at
room temperature. Wrap them in foil and
rewarm in a 350°F oven, if desired.

⅓ cup cake flour

¼ teaspoon baking soda

½ cup pure maple syrup

⅓ cup sour cream

¼ cup sugar

2 large eggs

Pinch of salt

1 cup wheat bran

4 tablespoons (½ stick) unsalted butter,
melted

A strong coffee and a freshly baked madeleine . . . *c'est parfait*! After making thousands of these buttery little French cakes over the course of my career in restaurants, I'm finally sharing my secret recipe for the perfect madeleine, with a golden chewy crust and light, fluffy interior. The bran makes these a healthier muffin alternative, and the maple syrup adds sweet flavor.

1. Position a rack in the center of the oven and preheat the oven to 350°F. Generously butter 7 molds of a large madeleine pan.

2. In a small bowl, whisk the flour and baking soda to blend. In a medium bowl, whisk the maple syrup, sour cream, sugar, eggs, and salt to blend. Stir in the flour mixture. Mix in the wheat bran, then mix in the melted butter.

3. Spoon about 1½ tablespoons of the batter into each of the 7 buttered molds. Bake for about 10 minutes, or until the madeleines are puffed and beginning to brown on the bottom. Immediately remove the madeleines from the pan and transfer to a cooling rack. Repeat to make the remaining madeleines, letting the pan cool and buttering it again before the second batch.

4. Serve the madeleines warm.

MADELEINE PANS

Madeleines are a little diva-ish—they require a special pan with shell-shaped molds—but the result is beautiful. You can pick up a madeleine pan for less than 15 bucks—treat yourself, and you'll find yourself making these little cakes often. If you're not sold just yet, remember, you can bake madeleine-shaped muffins with any muffin batter.

Yogurt Parfaits with Blackberries and Vanilla

Parfaits are quick and easy to assemble, so why not make a big batch and stick them in the fridge, ready to eat on the run. Treat yourself to fresh beautiful berries and a thick creamy yogurt for parfaits that are a cut above the store-bought kind.

SERVES: 4

PREP TIME: 5 minutes, plus 35 minutes to macerate the berries

MAKE-AHEAD: The parfaits will keep for up to 3 days, covered and refrigerated.

½ vanilla bean, split lengthwise

¼ cup sugar

2 cups fresh blackberries (about 12 ounces)

1 cinnamon stick

2⅔ cups plain yogurt

1. Using a paring knife, scrape the seeds from the vanilla bean into a medium bowl. Add the scraped bean and the sugar. Using your fingers, work the vanilla seeds into the sugar for about 1 minute, or until the mixture becomes delightfully fragrant. Add the blackberries and cinnamon and toss to combine. Set the berries aside at room temperature to macerate, stirring occasionally, for at least 35 minutes and up to 1 hour, or until they have released some of their juices and the sugar has dissolved.

2. Discard the cinnamon stick and divide the blackberries among four 10-ounce jars, glasses, or bowls. Spoon ⅔ cup of yogurt on top of the blackberry mixture in each jar. Enjoy immediately, or cover and refrigerate.

FOR A NICE CRUNCH

Spoon some golden granola (see page 187) on top of a parfait just before eating it. I add it at the last minute to prevent the granola from getting soggy. If you don't have granola on hand, you can use whatever cereal you have—you'll still get that satisfying crunch.

Croque Madame

SERVES: 4

PREP TIME: 5 minutes

COOK TIME: 15 minutes

MAKE-AHEAD: The Mornay sauce can be made up to 2 days ahead, cooled, covered, and refrigerated. Rewarm in a heavy saucepan over medium heat, stirring, for about 3 minutes and adding more milk to thin the sauce to the desired consistency, if necessary.

MORNAY SAUCE

2 tablespoons (¼ stick) unsalted butter

2 tablespoons all-purpose flour

1½ cups whole milk

½ cup grated Gruyère cheese

1 tablespoon Dijon mustard

Pinch of freshly grated nutmeg

Kosher salt and freshly ground white pepper

CROQUE MADAME

2 tablespoons (¼ stick) unsalted butter

4 ¾-inch-thick slices pain de mie (see Note, page 202)

½ cup grated Gruyère cheese

8 slices Black Forest ham

4 large eggs

Bring your knife and fork to the table for this classic French ham and cheese sandwich, because things are about to get messy. A croque madame is a croque monsieur with a fried egg plonked on top of it. Apparently it acquired its "madame" title because the sunny-side-up egg resembles a lady's hat—although it doesn't keep its form for long when I'm around to destroy it.

---

1. To make the Mornay sauce, in a medium heavy saucepan, melt the butter over medium-high heat. Stir in the flour and cook, stirring frequently, for about 2 minutes, or until the butter and flour are well blended and beginning to smell toasted. Gradually stir in half of the milk, and bring the mixture to a boil, stirring constantly to prevent lumps. Stir in the remaining milk and bring back to a boil, stirring constantly. Simmer, stirring, for 3 minutes, or until the sauce has thickened. Remove from the heat and stir in the Gruyère until melted. Stir in the Dijon mustard and nutmeg and season with salt and pepper. Cover to keep the sauce warm.

2. To make the croque madame, preheat the broiler. Line a heavy baking sheet with foil.

3. In a large heavy skillet, heat ½ tablespoon of the butter over medium heat until bubbly. Add 2 pieces of bread to the pan and toast for about 3 minutes per side, or until golden brown. Transfer the bread to the prepared baking sheet. Repeat with the remaining 2 pieces of bread, using another ½ tablespoon of the butter.

4. Divide half of the Gruyère among the toasts. Top each with 2 slices of ham and then scatter the remaining cheese on top of the ham. Broil the toasts for about 3 minutes, or until the cheese is browned and bubbling. Transfer the sandwiches to plates.

5. Meanwhile, in a large heavy nonstick skillet, melt ½ tablespoon of the butter over medium-high heat. Crack 2 eggs into the skillet and fry for about 3 minutes, or until the egg whites have set and the yolks have thickened but not set. Place 1 sunny-side-up egg on each sandwich.

(continued)

Repeat with the remaining 2 eggs, using the remaining ½ tablespoon butter for each egg.

6. Pour the warm Mornay sauce evenly over the toasts and serve immediately.

PAIN DE MIE

This French bread, called a Pullman loaf in the States, is a rectangular loaf of white sandwich bread with a fine-grained texture. Pain de mie toasts up well but other high-quality white sandwich bread, or even sliced French bread, can be substituted here.

Brekky Bagel Sandwich

There is nothing worse than a dry sandwich: I've laid on the moisture here in the form of provolone cheese, spicy mayonnaise, and a sunny-side-up egg. When you take your first bite, the yolk explodes through the hole in the bagel—it's a delicious sight to see. I want this messy sandwich on every birthday and Father's Day morning for the rest of my life. The meats I've selected below are ones that I usually have in my fridge, but you can use whatever cured or deli meats you have on hand. Frying them up gives them a nice crispy bite and releases more of their savory flavor.

SERVES: 2

PREP TIME: 5 minutes

COOK TIME: 10 minutes

MAKE-AHEAD: The spicy mayonnaise can be made up to 3 days ahead, covered, and refrigerated.

¼ cup Aïoli (page 30) or purchased mayonnaise

1 tablespoon Asian chile-garlic sauce (such as Sriracha)

2 teaspoons canola oil

4 slices capocollo

4 slices Genoa salami

4 slices smoked ham

2 tablespoons (¼ stick) unsalted butter

2 everything bagels, split

2 slices prosciutto

4 slices provolone cheese

2 large eggs

1. Preheat the oven to 400°F.

2. In a small bowl, mix the mayonnaise and chile sauce until smooth. Set aside.

3. In a large heavy skillet, heat the oil over medium-high heat until hot. Working in batches, cook the capocollo, salami, and ham for about 2 minutes per side, or until the edges are crisp. Transfer the meats to a plate.

4. Add 1 tablespoon of the butter to the pan and heat over medium heat until bubbly. Add the bagel halves to the pan, cut side down, and cook for about 3 minutes, or until golden brown. Transfer the bottom halves to a baking sheet, toasted side up, and put the top halves on a plate.

5. Spread the spicy mayonnaise over all the toasted bagel halves. Put half of the cooked meats and the prosciutto on each of the bottom halves and top with the cheese. Bake the sandwiches (without the tops) for about 3 minutes, or until the cheese is melted.

6. Meanwhile, in a medium heavy nonstick skillet, melt the remaining 1 tablespoon butter over medium heat. Crack the eggs into the pan and cook for about 3 minutes, or until the egg whites have set and the yolks have thickened but not set.

7. Remove the sandwiches from the oven and top each with an egg. Place the top halves of the bagels on top and serve immediately.

Crumpets

MAKES: 20 crumpets

PREP TIME: 10 minutes, plus 1½ hours for
the batter to rise

COOK TIME: 50 minutes

MAKE-AHEAD: The crumpets can be made
up to 3 days ahead and stored airtight at
room temperature.

1 cup whole milk, heated to 110° to 115°F

1 teaspoon sugar

1 tablespoon active dry yeast

1½ cups all-purpose flour

1 teaspoon kosher salt

⅓ cup water

½ teaspoon baking soda

Nonstick vegetable oil cooking spray

Crumpets are breakfast breads with a smooth bottom and a top riddled with air bubbles, perfect for soaking up jams, honey, and syrup. Similar in size to an English muffin, the batter is poured into stainless steel crumpet rings (find rings online for a couple of dollars or substitute ring molds) and cooked in a skillet. My brother, Luke, and I were crumpet fiends when we were younger, and we would smother them with butter and Vegemite. These days, I top my crumpets with the blackberry mixture from my yogurt parfaits (see page 199), the melted raspberries from morning toast (see page 179), Quick Mixed Berry Jam (page 165), or even Maple-Kumquat Syrup (page 190).

1. In the bowl of a stand mixer, mix the milk, sugar, and yeast. Set aside for 5 minutes, or until the mixture is frothy.

2. Attach the bowl to the mixer stand and, using the whisk attachment, mix the milk-yeast mixture with the flour and salt and then whisk on medium-high speed for about 3 minutes, or until the batter is thoroughly blended and stretches when you lift up the whisk. Remove the bowl from the mixer stand, cover tightly with plastic wrap, and let the batter rise in a warm, draft-free area for about 1 hour, or until the mixture is bubbly and has doubled in size.

3. In a small bowl, mix the water and baking soda. Stir the mixture into the batter and set aside for about 30 minutes, or until the batter is bubbly.

4. Heat a large heavy nonstick skillet over medium-low heat. Lightly spray the bottom of the pan and four 2½-inch crumpet molds or stainless steel ring molds with nonstick cooking spray and place the molds in the pan. Add 1½ tablespoons of batter to the center of each mold and cook for about 9 minutes, or until the bottoms are deep golden brown, air bubbles have formed on the tops, and the sides and tops of the crumpets have set. Using tongs, carefully remove the molds and, if desired, turn the crumpets over and cook for 1 minute to brown the other side. Transfer the crumpets to a plate and repeat with the remaining batter. Serve warm.

Chapter 6

SNACKS

EVEN WHEN I EAT A GOOD breakfast, lunch, and dinner, I need delicious little things to keep me going in between, in the "mids"— that is, midmorning, midafternoon, and midnight. After a run around the lake, a red-eye flight, or service at the restaurant, a snack attack strikes.

"Snacking" has *almost* become a dirty word because of the plethora of junk foods that tempt us from vending machines, at newsstands and gas stations . . . They're everywhere, and I have a bloody hard time trying to resist them! That's why I like to surround myself with plenty of better choices that are home-made and bursting with flavor (not with preservatives). My snacks can be as simple as a few slices of Bosc pear topped with a knob of Gorgonzola or a handful of roasted in-the-shell peanuts to crack while I tend to the veggie garden, but I also crave bites that are a little more elaborate and delicious.

I've put together a varied collection of my favorite things to snack on in this chapter, including fresh and healthy stuff like Bruschetta with Spring Pea Pesto and Burrata, and Grilled Flatbreads with Garlic-Rosemary Oil to pair with a luscious Roasted Beet Dip—honestly, I make this dip just to see that glorious deep magenta color come to life when the beets are mixed with yogurt, not to mention their unique earthy flavor. I have shared a couple of decadent recipes too, because sometimes snacks should be a fun treat, es-pecially when you're balancing them with nutritious meals. And I mean business—popcorn cooked with bacon and finished with a good coating of grated Parmesan cheese, and my mum's Chocolate Salted Caramel Kisses. She used to sneak these chewy-sticky caramels into my lunch box for me to stum-ble across. I reckon she made them in the dead of night while my brother, Luke, and I were asleep, because I always got a surprise when I found a "kiss" tucked underneath my sandwich.

One of the keys to snacking well is organization. Think about what you'd like to eat for the week ahead and add the ingredients to your shopping list. Once you've got the ingredients sorted and a couple of easy dishes in your repertoire, you'll be a step ahead when those "mids" sneak up on you.

Smoked Salmon Tartines with Red Onion–Caper Relish

There's something so appealing about open-faced sandwiches that most European countries have their own name for them. They're a snack I turn to often because I can take a slice of whatever bread I have on hand and top it with any bits of meat, cheese, relish, or spreads lying about in my fridge. This version is similar to what the Danish call *smørrebrød* (approximate pronunciation is "*smuhr*-bruth," but English speakers have a tough time saying the word correctly, so I use the French term for them, *tartines*). Slices of dense pumpernickel bread and French baguette are topped with a tangy cream cheese mixture and thin slices of smoked salmon and finished with a punchy relish. They're special enough to serve when friends come round, with a creamy Champagne or Chenin Blanc.

1. To make the relish, in a small bowl, stir the onion, capers, lemon juice, dill, and mustard seeds together. Season to taste with salt. Set aside.

2. To make the sandwiches, in another small bowl, mix the cream cheese, crème fraîche, and chives to blend. Season to taste with salt.

3. Spread the cheese mixture over the toasted slices of pumpernickel and baguette. Cut each slice of pumpernickel bread on the diagonal in half. Top each piece of bread with 1 salmon slice and then with a generous spoonful of the relish.

4. Transfer the tartines to a platter. Using a Microplane grater, finely grate the zest of the lemon over them and serve immediately.

SERVES: 8

PREP TIME: 25 minutes

COOK TIME: 8 minutes (to toast the bread)

MAKE-AHEAD: The cream cheese mixture can be made up to 1 day ahead, covered, and refrigerated. The relish can be made up to 4 hours ahead, covered, and refrigerated.

RELISH

½ cup finely diced red onion

¼ cup drained capers

1½ tablespoons fresh lemon juice

1 tablespoon chopped fresh dill

1 teaspoon yellow mustard seeds

Kosher salt

TARTINES

8 ounces cream cheese, at room temperature

⅓ cup crème fraîche or sour cream

¼ cup chopped fresh chives

Kosher salt

8 thin slices Danish-style pumpernickel bread (about 3½ x 3½ x ¼ inch), toasted

16 thin slices French baguette, toasted

1 pound thinly sliced smoked salmon

1 lemon

Manchego Crackers

MAKES: about 36 3 x 2-inch crackers

PREP TIME: 10 minutes

COOK TIME: 15 minutes

MAKE-AHEAD: The crackers will keep for up to 3 days, stored airtight at room temperature.

¾ cup all-purpose flour

1½ cups finely grated Manchego cheese (about 3½ ounces)

¼ teaspoon baking powder

¼ teaspoon kosher salt

¼ cup water

2 tablespoons plus 2 teaspoons extra-virgin olive oil

½ teaspoon fleur de sel

Cheese and crackers is the quintessential snack. Here I've combined the two into one crisp, cheesy cracker, and while there is certainly an overwhelming amount of crackers sold in the stores, I don't believe any stand up to the taste and freshness of this one. Manchego is a firm, sweet, and nutty Spanish sheep's-milk cheese that melts well. Most of it is grated and incorporated into the dough here, and the remaining cheese is sprinkled on top of it, which is baked as one big cracker. Once baked, roughly break for a rustic, relaxed feel and serve with an antipasto or charcuterie platter. For herbed crackers, throw a few pinches of chopped fresh rosemary or thyme into the food processor and pulse with the dough.

1. Preheat the oven to 375°F.

2. In a food processor, combine the flour, 1 cup of the cheese, the baking powder, and the kosher salt and process to blend. Add the water and 2 tablespoons of the oil and pulse until a moist, crumbly dough forms.

3. Roll out the dough very thin on the back of a 17 x 11-inch baking sheet so it completely covers the baking sheet. Using a fork, prick the dough all over. Rub the remaining 2 teaspoons oil over the dough and then sprinkle the remaining ½ cup cheese and the fleur de sel over it.

4. Bake for about 15 minutes, or until the cracker is a pale golden color. Cool completely on the baking sheet, then break into pieces.

SNAP!

It's important that the dough for this cracker is rolled out super thin in order to give you a good snappy cracker. But I promise you, it's not difficult to do. The dough is rolled out over the bottom of a baking sheet until it entirely covers the sheet, so there's no guessing about how much to roll it out. More importantly, there are no worries about the dough sticking to the counter or transferring the rolled dough to the baking sheet.

Mulita-Style Quesadillas

Mulitas are Mexican corn tortilla sandwiches filled with your choice of cheese and meat, then pan-fried until they are crisp on the outside and the cheese has melted. It's a great way to use up leftover braised, grilled, or roasted meats. For a heartier snack or light meal, serve the quesadillas with a bowl of the Humble Beans (page 113)

SERVES: 6

PREP TIME: 10 minutes

COOK TIME: 12 minutes

2 cups shredded Monterey Jack cheese (about 6 ounces)

1 cup crumbled queso fresco (3 ounces)

12 corn tortillas

1½ cups diced roasted pork belly (see page 55) or grilled rib-eye steak (see page 62) or shredded Porcini-Braised Beef with Horseradish Mascarpone (page 65)

¼ cup coarsely chopped fresh cilantro

6 tablespoons canola oil

Kosher salt

1 cup Mouth-on-Fire Salsa (page 220)

½ cup sour cream

2 limes, cut into wedges

1. In a small bowl, mix the cheeses together. Top each of 6 tortillas with ¼ cup of the cheese mixture, ¼ cup of the meat, and another ¼ cup of the cheese mixture. Sprinkle with the cilantro and top with the remaining 6 tortillas. Press down gently on the quesadillas to compress them.

2. Heat a large griddle or skillet over medium-low heat. Add 3 tablespoons of the oil, then add 3 of the quesadillas and cook for about 3 minutes per side, or until they are golden brown and crisp on the outside and the cheese has melted. Transfer the quesadillas to plates and sprinkle with salt. Wipe out the pan and cook the remaining 3 quesadillas, using the remaining 3 tablespoons oil.

3. Serve the quesadillas immediately with the salsa, sour cream, and lime wedges.

VARIATION I also love to make quesadillas without the meat, adding a fresh cabbage slaw instead. While the quesadillas cook, mix 2 cups finely shredded green cabbage, ¼ cup coarsely chopped fresh cilantro, and ¼ cup finely diced white onion. When the quesadillas are hot out of the pan, open them up and tuck in the slaw upon serving.

Homemade Tortilla Chips with Mouth-on-Fire Salsa

MAKES: 60 chips (about 8 cups)

PREP TIME: 5 minutes

COOK TIME: 12 minutes

MAKE-AHEAD: The chips will keep for up to 3 days stored in an airtight container at room temperature. You can rewarm them in a 250°F oven, if desired.

Canola oil for deep-frying

15 corn tortillas

Kosher salt

Mouth-on-Fire Salsa (recipe follows)

I remember making corn chips for my nephews one day and them saying, "You mean it's just frying pieces of corn tortillas in oil?!" Use your hands to tear the tortillas for rough-around-the-edges corn chips and fry them until they reach a deep golden color so they'll be crunchy and tasty. If they're too pale, they'll be chewy and lack that toasty flavor.

1. Pour 3 inches of oil into a large heavy pot and heat over medium-high heat to 350°F. Meanwhile, tear each tortilla in half, and then tear the halves in half.

2. Working in batches, cook the tortilla chips in the hot oil, stirring nearly constantly with a spider or slotted spoon, for about 3 minutes, or until golden and crispy. Use the spider to remove the chips from the oil and transfer to a baking sheet lined with paper towels. Season immediately with salt to taste. Repeat with the remaining tortillas.

3. Serve the chips with the salsa.

A SPIDER?

A spider is a wide, shallow wire-mesh basket with a long wooden handle. It's a handy utensil to have by your side in the kitchen—you can use it to lift and drain foods from soups, stocks, water, or oil.

Mouth-on-Fire Salsa

My friend Michael Torres showed me how to make this salsa. It's a staple he always has in his fridge, and now I do too. His tip: "Make sure the veggies and peppers are *quemada*!" That's right, go beyond merely charring them to basically burning the outside of them (*quemada* means "burnt" in Spanish). It's what gives this salsa its incredibly rich, smoky, intense flavor. You'll find yourself dousing everything with it—a pan of scrambled eggs, a grilled rib-eye steak (see page 62), a sandwich made with leftover Braised Pork with Spicy Chipotle Sauce (page 58), Mulita-Style Quesadillas (page 217)—and your chips and salsa will be taken to a whole new level. If you want to go crazy, add a chipotle chile to the blender. Alternatively, if you want to tone down the heat, remove the seeds from the jalapeños and reduce the amount of chiles de árbol, or omit them. The salsa will keep for up to 5 days, stored airtight in the refrigerator.

MAKES: 4 cups

3 tablespoons olive oil
2 dried chiles de árbol
8 large tomatillos, husked and rinsed
3 medium heirloom tomatoes (about 1¼ pounds)
2 red jalapeño peppers
1 green jalapeño pepper
1 bunch scallions, trimmed
Juice of 1 lemon
2 garlic cloves
1 cup coarsely chopped fresh cilantro
Kosher salt

1. Prepare a grill for high heat.

2. In a small heavy sauté pan, combine the oil and chiles de árbol and cook over medium heat for about 4 minutes, or until the chiles are toasted and beginning to blacken. Remove the chiles and set aside. Allow the chile oil to cool slightly.

3. On a large baking sheet, toss the tomatillos, tomatoes, jalapeños, and scallions with the chile oil and season with salt. Lightly oil the grill grates, place the vegetables on the grill, and close the lid. Cook the vegetables, turning only once, until they are blackened as much as possible; don't stress out if the tomatoes and tomatillos break open and begin to fall apart—it's a sign that they're cooked through. Aim for these cooking times: 8 minutes per side for the tomatoes and tomatillos, about 6 minutes per side for the jalapeños, and about 3 minutes per side for the scallions. Using tongs, transfer the vegetables to the baking sheet and let cool slightly.

4. Trim the stems from the jalapeños and remove the seeds, if desired. Do not remove the charred skin.

5. In a blender, combine the blackened vegetables, the garlic, cilantro, lemon juice, and toasted chiles de árbol and blend until smooth. Season the salsa to taste with salt.

Popcorn with Bacon and Parmesan

I made this for the first time when my mate, the big man Carlos, came over to watch a game. I'd fried up some bacon that morning and when I looked over at the leftover fat, I thought, "Hmm, I wonder if that could work with popcorn." It more than worked: Carlos went mad for it. He was scooping it out of the bowl, talking with his mouth full, saying, "Man, this is freaking amazing! We've got to package this." But, of course, the beauty of this snack is its freshness and the warm melted cheese. He's right . . . this popcorn is off the charts.

SERVES: 6 (makes 8 cups of popped popcorn)
PREP TIME: 5 minutes
COOK TIME: 10 minutes

6 slices bacon (about 6 ounces), finely chopped
2 tablespoons canola oil
½ cup organic popcorn kernels
1¼ teaspoons kosher salt
1 1½-ounce piece Parmesan cheese

1. Heat a large heavy skillet over medium-high heat. Add the bacon and cook, stirring as the fat renders, for about 5 minutes, or until the bacon is crisp. Using a slotted spoon, transfer the bacon to a plate lined with paper towels. Pour the bacon fat into a small bowl, leaving the brown solids behind. Reserve the bacon fat.

2. Heat a large heavy pot over medium-high heat until hot. Add the oil and popcorn kernels and cover the pot. Once the kernels begin to pop, using pot holders, shake the pan constantly over the heat as the kernels pop for about 5 minutes, or until all the kernels have popped.

3. In a large bowl, toss the popcorn with the bacon, reserved bacon fat, and the salt. Using a Microplane grater, finely grate most of the Parmesan over the popcorn and toss to coat. Grate more cheese on top and serve immediately.

Grilled Cheese Toasts

MAKES: 12 slices cheese bread (and about 1 cup cheese spread)

PREP TIME: 5 minutes

COOK TIME: 3 minutes

MAKE-AHEAD: The cheese-butter spread will keep for up to 2 weeks, covered, and refrigerated.

2 ounces extra-sharp Cheddar cheese

2 ounces Parmesan cheese

12 tablespoons (1½ sticks) unsalted butter, at room temperature

1½ teaspoons garlic powder

¼ teaspoon sweet paprika

Kosher salt and freshly ground black pepper

12 slices sourdough bread

3 tablespoons finely chopped fresh chives

For these toasts, Parmesan cheese, extra-sharp Cheddar, paprika, garlic powder, and butter are combined in a food processor and spread over slices of sourdough bread, and then broiled. The cheese bread makes a great sandwich substitute or soup accompaniment, and the spread works brilliantly on meats, veggies, or baked potatoes.

1. Preheat the broiler. Fit a food processor with the shredding blade and shred the cheeses. Replace the shredding blade with the regular (S-shaped) blade. If necessary, remove the cheese to change the blade, then return the cheese to the processor before proceeding. Add the butter, garlic powder, and paprika and process until creamy, with small bits of cheese still visible. Season to taste with salt and pepper.

2. Spread about 1½ tablespoons of the cheese mixture over each slice of bread and arrange them on a baking sheet. Broil for about 3 minutes, or until the topping bubbles and turns golden brown. Sprinkle with the chives and serve immediately.

Roasted Beet Dip

Branch out from the dips that you're used to and go a little beet crazy. Dukkah and homemade flatbreads go perfectly with this luscious, earthy dip. I usually chuck a couple of extra beets onto the baking sheet, then refrigerate them and slice for salads and sandwiches during the week.

MAKES: 3 cups

PREP TIME: 10 minutes

COOK TIME: 45 minutes

MAKE-AHEAD: The beet dip can be made up to 2 days ahead, covered, and refrigerated.

1. Preheat the oven to 400°F.

2. In an 8-inch square baking dish, toss the beets with the olive oil to coat and season with salt and pepper. Add ¼ cup water and cover the pan tightly with foil. Roast for about 45 minutes, or until the beets are tender. Allow the beets to cool for 10 minutes.

3. Using paper towels, rub the beets to remove their skins (the skins will slip right off). Cut enough of the beets into about ¼-inch dice to measure 1 cup; reserve the trimmings. Set the diced beets aside.

4. Quarter the remaining beets and combine in a food processor with the beet trimmings and garlic and process until finely chopped. Add the yogurt, extra-virgin olive oil, and lemon juice and blend to a smooth puree. Season with salt and pepper. Transfer the mixture to a medium bowl and fold in the diced beets.

5. To serve, transfer the beet dip to a serving bowl and sprinkle some of the dukkah evenly over it. Serve the flatbreads and remaining dukkah alongside for dipping.

4 medium red beets
(about 1 pound total), trimmed

1 tablespoon olive oil

Kosher salt and freshly ground black pepper

1 garlic clove

1½ cups plain Greek yogurt

¼ cup extra-virgin olive oil

1 tablespoon fresh lemon juice

½ cup Dukkah (recipe follows)

Grilled Flatbreads with Garlic-Rosemary Oil (page 230) or 4 pita breads

Dukkah

Dukkah is an Egyptian spice blend loaded with a unique combination of coarsely ground toasted seeds and nuts. For a simple snack, dip a piece of pita bread or grilled flatbread (see page 230) into extra-virgin olive oil, or your favorite dip, then dunk it into dukkah. Sprinkle dukkah on deviled eggs or over a green salad, and use it as a crust for fish, chicken, or lamb chops. It will keep for up to 1 week, stored airtight at room temperature.

MAKES: 1½ cups

½ cup hazelnuts
¼ cup sliced almonds
⅓ cup coriander seeds
⅓ cup white sesame seeds
2 tablespoons cumin seeds
1 teaspoon fennel seeds
½ teaspoon kosher salt
¼ teaspoon freshly ground black pepper
¼ teaspoon cayenne pepper

1. Preheat the oven to 400°F.

2. Spread the hazelnuts and almonds on separate small baking pans and toast in the oven until fragrant and golden, stirring occasionally, about 8 minutes for the hazelnuts and 6 minutes for the almonds.

3. Rub the warm hazelnuts in a cloth to remove the brown skins. Cool the hazelnuts and almonds completely.

4. Heat a small heavy sauté pan over medium heat. Add the coriander seeds and stir for about 3 minutes, or until aromatic and toasted. Transfer to a small plate and set aside. Add the sesame seeds, cumin seeds, and fennel seeds to the pan and stir over medium heat for about 3 minutes, or until toasted and aromatic. Transfer to a plate and cool completely.

5. In a food processor, pulse the coriander seeds four times to break them up. Add the hazelnuts, almonds, sesame seeds, cumin seeds, and fennel seeds and pulse until coarsely ground; the mixture should be the texture of coarse bread crumbs. Do not blend to a paste.

6. Transfer to a bowl and stir in the salt, black pepper, and cayenne.

Grilled Flatbreads with Garlic-Rosemary Oil

SERVES: 8

PREP TIME: 15 minutes, plus 45 minutes for the dough to rise.

COOK TIME: 15 minutes

MAKE-AHEAD: The flatbreads can be made up to 1 day ahead and stored airtight at room temperature. To reheat, wrap them in foil and warm in a 350°F oven.

GARLIC-ROSEMARY OIL

⅔ cup extra-virgin olive oil

1 garlic clove, finely chopped

1 shallot, finely chopped

1 fresh rosemary sprig

Kosher salt and freshly ground black pepper

FLATBREADS

1 cup warm water (110° to 115°F)

2¼ teaspoons active dry yeast

2 teaspoons sugar

2⅔ cups all-purpose flour, plus more for dusting

2 teaspoons kosher salt

Enjoy these grilled flatbreads with dips and serve alongside soups or classic Italian dishes to mop up those silky tomato sauces. Alternatively, the flatbreads can be baked—instructions follow.

1. To make the garlic-rosemary oil, in a small saucepan, combine the oil, garlic, shallot, and rosemary and heat over low heat for about 10 minutes, or until fragrant. Remove the saucepan from the heat and season the oil to taste with salt and pepper.

2. To prepare the flatbread dough, in a small bowl, stir the warm water, yeast, and sugar to blend. Set aside for about 5 minutes, or until foamy.

3. In a food processor, combine the flour and salt and process to blend. With the machine running, add the yeast mixture and 1 tablespoon of the garlic oil and process just until the dough comes together. Transfer the dough to a work surface and knead until smooth and elastic.

4. Divide the dough into 8 pieces (about 3 ounces each) and shape into balls. Place the dough balls on an oiled baking sheet and rub them lightly with some of the garlic oil. Cover with a piece of oiled plastic wrap and let rise in a warm, draft-free spot for about 45 minutes, or until doubled in size.

5. To shape and grill the flatbreads, prepare a grill for medium-high heat. Lightly oil the grill grates.

6. Using a rolling pin, roll each dough ball out on a floured work surface into a thin 11 x 5-inch oval (the shape does not have to be perfect). Set them aside on the oiled baking sheet.

7. Working in batches, brush the flatbreads with some of the garlic oil and lay them on the grill grate. Grill for about 2 minutes per side, or until grill marks form and the bread is cooked through. Wrap the breads in a clean kitchen towel to keep them warm.

8. To serve, brush the flatbreads with more of the garlic oil, if desired, and serve with any remaining oil for dipping.

VARIATION Baked Flatbreads Position a rack in the lower third of the oven and set a pizza stone on the rack. Preheat the oven to 500°F. Working with one piece of dough at a time, roll the dough out as directed above. Lightly brush the top of the flatbreads with garlic oil and drape the flatbreads, oiled side down, over the stone. Bake for about 5 minutes, or until golden brown on the bottom and baked through. Wrap the breads in a clean kitchen towel to keep them warm and serve as above.

Bruschetta with Spring Pea Pesto and Burrata

Pulsing just half of the peas and folding in the rest whole gives you a lovely, textural pesto with clean, bright flavors. It's a nice afternoon snack or pre-dinner bite, or transform it into a meal by tossing the pesto and some roughly chopped burrata with spaghetti and serve the ciabatta on the side.

SERVES: 4

PREP TIME: 20 minutes

COOK TIME: 8 minutes

1 cup loosely packed fresh basil leaves

1 cup loosely packed fresh mint leaves

8 tablespoons extra-virgin olive oil

1½ teaspoons grated lemon zest

1 tablespoon fresh lemon juice

Kosher salt

4 ½-inch-thick slices ciabatta bread

1 small shallot, finely chopped

1 garlic clove, finely chopped

1½ cups shelled fresh English peas (from 1½ pounds peas in the pod)

4 ounces burrata or fresh mozzarella, at room temperature

Freshly ground black pepper

2 tablespoons freshly grated Parmesan cheese

1. Preheat the oven to 350°F.

2. In a small food processor, combine the basil, mint, 5 tablespoons of the oil, the lemon zest, and juice and process until nearly smooth. Season to taste with salt. Leave the mixture in the food processor.

3. Heat a grill pan over medium-high heat. Drizzle 1 tablespoon of the oil over the ciabatta and season with salt. Grill the ciabatta for about 3 minutes per side, or until lightly toasted and grill marks form. Transfer to a plate.

4. Heat a medium heavy skillet over medium heat. Add the remaining 2 tablespoons oil, then add the shallot and garlic and sauté for about 2 minutes, or until tender and translucent. Add the peas and cook for about 5 minutes, or until they are cooked through but still crisp-tender. Remove from the heat.

5. Add half of the warm pea mixture to the pesto and pulse until the peas are coarsely chopped. Transfer the mixture to a bowl and fold in the remaining warm pea mixture. Season with salt.

6. Divide the burrata among the bruschetta and season with salt and pepper. Spoon the pesto over, sprinkle with the Parmesan, and serve immediately.

Lemongrass Chicken Wings

SERVES: 4

PREP TIME: 10 minutes, plus 2 hours for marinating the chicken

COOK TIME: 10 minutes

MAKE-AHEAD: The chicken can be marinated for up to 2 days.

12 whole chicken wings

1 cup plus 1 tablespoon Green Curry Paste (recipe follows)

1 tablespoon butter, at room temperature

Chopped fresh cilantro, for garnish

1 lime, cut into wedges

The longer it marinates, the more flavor the chicken takes on. Fire up the grill or broiler and cook as many as you need to satisfy that snack craving—double or triple the recipe for larger groups. Or as part of a meal, use chicken drumsticks, thighs, or breasts instead of wings and adjust the cooking time accordingly.

1. Cut the chicken wings through the center joint to separate the drummettes. Transfer to a large bowl.

2. Rub the chicken with 1 cup of the curry paste to coat. Cover and marinate in the refrigerator for at least 2 hours.

3. Prepare a grill for medium heat. Oil the grill grate.

4. Grill the chicken wings for about 10 minutes, turning as needed, or until slightly charred and cooked through. In a bowl, toss the chicken with the remaining 1 tablespoon curry paste and butter to coat. Transfer to a platter, sprinkle with cilantro, and serve immediately with lime wedges.

Green Curry Paste

Use this Thai paste as a marinade, in stir-fries or curries, and as a soup base. It will keep for up to 5 days, stored in an airtight container in the refrigerator.

MAKES: 2 cups

2 teaspoons coriander seeds

⅔ cup packed fresh cilantro leaves

⅓ cup packed fresh basil leaves

2 large shallots, peeled and quartered

8 garlic cloves

2 lemongrass stalks, trimmed to 8 inches and thinly sliced

1 4-inch piece fresh ginger, peeled and coarsely chopped

4 Thai chiles or small serrano chiles, coarsely chopped

2 kaffir lime leaves, coarsely chopped

2 tablespoons fish sauce

¼ cup canola oil

1. Heat a small heavy sauté pan over medium heat. Add the coriander seeds and stir for about 3 minutes, or until toasted. Transfer the coriander seeds to a plate to cool.

2. In a small food processor, combine the coriander seeds, cilantro, basil, shallots, garlic, lemongrass, ginger, chiles, and lime leaves and process, stopping occasionally to scrape down the sides of the bowl, until very finely chopped. Add the fish sauce and oil and process, stopping occasionally to scrape down the sides of the processor, until a coarse paste forms.

Sesame Shrimp Toast with Sweet Chile Sauce

SERVES: 4

PREP TIME: 10 minutes

COOK TIME: 10 minutes

MAKE-AHEAD: The shrimp mixture can be
made up to 1 day ahead, covered, and
refrigerated.

8 ounces peeled and deveined small shrimp
(21 to 25 per pound)

2 tablespoons Green Curry Paste
(page 236) or purchased green curry paste

1 large egg yolk

½ teaspoon kosher salt, plus more
for seasoning

9 ¼-inch-thick slices white bread

½ cup white sesame seeds

Canola oil, for deep-frying

Sweet Chile Sauce (recipe follows; optional)

I like to kick back and enjoy these tasty toasts with a cold beer, but
they're also a great appetizer before a Thai salad. Or throw them on
top of a simple spinach salad, which will wilt from the heat in the most
delicious way. Here's another idea: make bite-size square toasts and
serve them as a casual hors d'oeuvre.

1. In a small food processor, combine the shrimp, curry paste, egg yolk,
   and salt and process until a smooth puree forms. Transfer the mixture
   to a bowl.

2. Trim the crusts from the bread, leaving rectangles that are 4 x 3 inches.
   Cut the bread slices lengthwise in half.

3. Spread 2 teaspoons of the shrimp mixture over each piece of bread.
   Sprinkle the sesame seeds heavily over the shrimp mixture so that the
   sesame seeds cover most of it.

4. Pour 3 inches of oil into a large heavy pot and heat over medium-high
   heat until the oil reaches 375°F. Add 4 of the toasts and fry, using a
   slotted spoon to keep the toasts submerged as much as possible, for
   about 1½ minutes, or until the bread is crisp and the sesame seeds are
   golden brown. Transfer the toasts to a wire rack set over a baking sheet
   to drain. Season lightly with salt. Repeat with the remaining toasts.

5. Serve with the sweet chile sauce, if desired.

Sweet Chile Sauce

Two minutes prep, 6 minutes cooking. It's quicker to whip this sauce up at home than run out to the store. Plus, you can adjust the amount of red pepper flakes to your liking, 'cuz, after all, some like it hot, baby! The sauce will keep for up to 5 days, stored airtight at room temperature.

MAKES: about 1 cup

1 cup sugar
½ cup rice vinegar
½ cup water
1 teaspoon red pepper flakes
1 teaspoon kosher salt

In a small saucepan, combine all of the ingredients and bring to a boil over medium-high heat, stirring to dissolve the sugar. Boil the sauce for 6 minutes, or until the sauce has reduced by one third, and remove from the heat.

Peanut Butter, Jam, and Banana Burrito to Go

SERVES: 1

PREP TIME: 5 minutes

COOK TIME: 1 minute

1 flour tortilla

3 tablespoons crunchy peanut butter

2 tablespoons plain Greek yogurt

2 tablespoons Quick Mixed Berry Jam (page 165) or your favorite jam

½ banana, thinly sliced

You wouldn't typically find an Aussie snacking on PB+J, but I make exceptions for this unusual burrito. There's a bit of everything going on here: a satisfying contrast of warm and cold, sweet and tangy flavors, and a subtle crunch. Yum.

1. Heat the tortilla directly on a gas burner for about 10 seconds per side, or until it is hot, softened, and slightly charred.

2. Spread the peanut butter over the tortilla (and watch it melt slightly), then top with the yogurt, jam, and banana. Quickly roll it up and eat immediately while it is still warm and oozing.

Chocolate-Hazelnut Milkshake

When you're feeling a little peckish, this milkshake really satisfies. It's rich with the chocolate-hazelnut spread, but nicely balanced by the (dairy-free) sorbet and almond milk.

SERVES: 2

PREP TIME: 15 minutes

In a blender, combine the almond milk, ice, and chocolate-hazelnut spread and blend well. Add the chocolate sorbet and blend until smooth. Pour into two tall glasses and serve.

1 cup Homemade Almond Milk (page 265)

1 cup ice cubes

1 cup chocolate-hazelnut spread (such as Nutella)

2 cups chocolate sorbet

Awesome Brownies

MAKES: 25 small brownies

PREP TIME: 10 minutes, plus cooling time

COOK TIME: 35 minutes

MAKE-AHEAD: The brownies can be made up to 1 day ahead, covered, and stored at room temperature.

Nonstick vegetable oil cooking spray

9 ounces bittersweet chocolate (61% cacao or less), chopped

11 tablespoons (1 stick plus 3 tablespoons) unsalted butter, cut into 1-inch cubes

1¼ cups sugar

3 large eggs

1½ teaspoons pure vanilla extract

¼ teaspoon salt

1 cup unbleached all-purpose flour

1½ cups pecans, toasted and coarsely chopped

Awesome brownies dreamt up by my even more awesome food editor, Rochelle Palermo. There's something pretty special about life when you have a cookie jar filled with Ro's brownies. And while other brownies are great, this one is king, with melted, gooey chocolate and crunchy toasted pecans sitting on top of the chocolatey base (yep, that's two chocolate injections in one dish). They're rich, so you'll want to cut them into small squares.

1. Position a rack in the center of the oven and preheat the oven to 350°F. Line a 9 x 9 x 2-inch baking pan with foil, leaving an overhang on two opposite sides. Spray the foil with nonstick cooking spray.

2. Combine two-thirds (6 ounces) of the chocolate and all the butter in a medium heatproof bowl, set the bowl over a saucepan of simmering water, and stir until the chocolate and butter are melted and smooth. Remove the bowl from the heat and cool for 5 to 10 minutes, or until the chocolate mixture is lukewarm.

3. In a large bowl, whisk the sugar, eggs, vanilla, and salt to blend. Whisk in the chocolate mixture. Stir in the flour, then stir in 1 cup of the pecans.

4. Transfer the batter to the prepared baking pan. Sprinkle the remaining chocolate and ½ cup pecans over the top. Bake the brownies for 28 to 30 minutes, or until a toothpick inserted into the center comes out with just a few moist crumbs attached. Transfer the pan to a cooling rack and let the brownies cool.

5. Using the foil as an aid, lift the brownie sheet from the pan. Fold down the foil edges. Using a large sharp knife, cut the brownie sheet into 25 squares, wiping the knife with a hot moist cloth after each cut. Transfer to an airtight container.

Chocolate Salted Caramel Kisses

MAKES: 20 kisses

PREP TIME: 20 minutes, plus 40 minutes
for cooling and chilling

COOK TIME: 20 minutes

MAKE-AHEAD: The kisses will keep for up
to 3 days, stored airtight in the refrigerator.

1 cup sugar

¼ cup water

½ cup heavy cream

1⅓ cups salted roasted cashews

Nonstick vegetable oil cooking spray

7 ounces bittersweet chocolate
(70% cacao), chopped

Drool alert: these roasted cashew nut clusters contain two of my all-time favorite ingredients: caramel and chocolate. They're bite-size, so you don't have to feel guilty about indulging in their deliciousness—simply savor every last little bit.

1. To make the caramel cashews, in a medium heavy saucepan, stir the sugar and water over medium-high heat until the sugar dissolves, occasionally brushing down the sides of the pan with a wet pastry brush to remove any sugar crystals. Then bring the sugar syrup to a boil, without stirring, and cook, brushing down the sides of the pan and swirling the pan occasionally to ensure the caramel cooks evenly, for about 8 minutes, or until the caramel is golden brown.

2. Remove the pan from the heat and mix in the cream; the caramel will bubble vigorously. Allow the caramel to cool for 15 minutes; it will thicken slightly.

3. Line two large baking sheets with parchment paper. Lightly spray the parchment paper on one baking sheet with nonstick cooking spray. Stir the cashews into the caramel to coat. Using two spoons, drop tablespoonfuls of the caramel-cashew mixture onto the sprayed baking sheet, forming about 20 small mounds. Refrigerate for about 15 minutes, or until the clusters are cold and the caramel is somewhat firmer.

4. Meanwhile, to make the coating, place the chocolate in a small heatproof bowl, set the bowl over a small saucepan of simmering water, and melt the chocolate, stirring often until smooth. Remove the bowl from the heat.

5. Using a small metal spatula, lift one cluster from the baking sheet and drop it into the melted chocolate, turning to coat completely. Using a fork, immediately lift the cluster out of the chocolate, gently shake the excess chocolate back into the bowl, and, using a second fork as an aid, place the kiss on the second prepared baking sheet. Repeat with the remaining clusters and melted chocolate.

6. Refrigerate the caramel kisses for at least 10 minutes, or until the chocolate is cold and set. Transfer to an airtight container and return to the refrigerator until ready to serve.

Chapter 7
DRINKS

———

MY FEELING IS THAT A MEAL is really not complete without something fantastic to drink. Pubs, bars, clubs, cafés, and teahouses wouldn't be thriving on every street corner if there weren't something more to them than just quenching thirst. People come together in these spots to celebrate, relax, do business, and if you're like me, catch a live game with a few mates.

When it comes to choosing beverages to serve at a meal, you need to think about the atmosphere you want to set and how your choice will complement the food (though, of course, some drinks, like a thick and heavenly Weeknight Belgian Hot Chocolate, are usually best savored on their own). Just imagine how different a time you are going to have if someone offers you Champagne or a Fresh Blackberry Cocktail as opposed to a cup of tea.

When people are coming round, I always like to have a cocktail or two that are really easy to prepare in batches, like Pineapple-Lime Margaritas or Spicy and Smoky Bloody Marys—how spicy can *you* take it? Half the fun comes from encouraging your guests to tailor their cocktails to their personal taste with garnishes, or an extra nip, as they desire. I usually enlist the help of a couple of friends to keep on top of making sure everyone is well-watered. As you can imagine, they end up having the best time going around chatting with everyone.

Since my beautiful girl, Linds, was pregnant last year with our second son, Emerson, and therefore on the wagon, I was able to perfect my recipe for lemonade. *And* because my appreciation for a good drink stretches beyond the boozed-up kind, I've also come up with some other nonalcoholic drinks— a Strawberry-Hibiscus Punch and an Italian Rhubarb-Orange Soda, with flavors unmatched by anything you'll find in a bottle. There is nothing more enticing than the smell of good coffee on a Sunday morning, so I decided I would master the art of brewing French Press Coffee at home. Because why not make every drink that passes our lips taste awesome?

Fresh Mint Tea

Simple? Absolutely. But once you've tried a cup of sweet-smelling fresh mint tea, it'll become your daily addiction. Both mint and steaming-hot water have calming properties that do wonders for your body. I like to slowly sip away just before bed for an out-for-the-count, wonderfully sound sleep.

1. Bring the filtered water to a boil in a teakettle or saucepan over high heat.

2. Place the mint sprigs in 2 teacups or mugs. Pour enough hot water over the mint to fill the cups or mugs and let steep for about 1 minute, swirling the water with the mint sprigs. Serve immediately.

MAKES: 4 cups

PREP TIME: 2 minutes

COOK TIME: 4 minutes

MAKE-AHEAD: The tea, of course, should be enjoyed while hot, but to serve it as iced mint tea, make a triple batch up to 4 hours ahead. Remove the mint sprigs after steeping for 2 minutes, then cover and refrigerate the tea until cold. Serve over ice.

About 4 cups filtered water
2 large fresh mint sprigs (about 12 to 14 leaves per sprig)

Strawberry-Hibiscus Punch

MAKES: 6 to 8 cups

PREP TIME: 5 minutes, plus 2 hours steeping time

COOK TIME: 2 minutes

MAKE-AHEAD: The punch can be made up to 5 days ahead, covered, and refrigerated.

6 to 8 cups filtered water

1 cup sugar

1 cup dried hibiscus (Jamaica) flowers

8 ounces fresh strawberries, hulled and sliced (2 cups), plus more for garnish

1 2-inch piece fresh ginger, thinly sliced

Ice cubes

With its deep, rosy red color and slightly sweet taste, this fruity punch is a far cry from a sugary kids' version, but they'll love it. Get your hands on dried hibiscus flowers (sold as Jamaica flowers or flor de Jamaica) at your local health food store or Latino market.

1. In a large heavy saucepan, combine 4 cups of the filtered water with the sugar and bring to a simmer over medium-high heat, stirring to dissolve the sugar.

2. Remove the pan from the heat and add the hibiscus flowers, strawberries, and ginger. (Be sure to pause and take note of how beautiful the mixture looks.) Steep for about 2 hours.

3. Strain the liquid into a bowl and stir in 2 to 4 cups of filtered water, depending on your taste. Transfer the punch to a pitcher. Serve over ice and garnish with more strawberries.

Hudson's Good Morning Juice

My son and I (along with the rest of Los Angeles and beyond) are a little juicing-obsessed. The first thing he says to me in the morning is, "Make juice, Dada?" We pick a few fresh greens from the garden, cut up some apples and celery, and make a healthy start to the day. Hud's fascinated by the fact that you put fruit and veggies in the top of the juicer and liquid dribbles out the bottom. I tell him there's a bunny in there chomping away, which sends him into a fit of excitement.

SERVES: 4

PREP TIME: 10 minutes

4 Granny Smith apples, quartered
4 Pink Lady apples, quartered
5 celery stalks, cut into 4 pieces each
2 cups loosely packed spinach leaves
1 cup loosely packed fresh mint leaves
3 tablespoons fresh lime juice
1 2-inch piece fresh ginger, peeled
Ice cubes, optional

1. With the motor running, feed all the ingredients except the ice into a juicer, catching the juices in a bowl.

2. Fill four glasses with the ice cubes, if desired, pour the juice over the ice, and enjoy immediately.

Lindsay's Lemonade

MAKES: 8 cups

PREP TIME: 10 minutes

MAKE-AHEAD: The lemonade can be made up to 2 days ahead, covered, and refrigerated.

5 lemons

1 cup sugar

7 cups cold filtered water

Ice cubes

When baby number one, Hudson, was on the way, Lindsay craved chunky guacamole. During her second pregnancy, with Emerson, all she could think about was her homemade lemonade. Pregnancy cravings aside, this classic lemonade is a lovely, thirst-quenching drink that everyone can enjoy.

1. Using a Microplane grater, finely grate the zest from the lemons (avoid the bitter white pith) into a bowl. Doing this over the bowl collects all the essential oils that will burst out of the zest as you grate it, giving you more lemon flavor in your lemonade. Add the sugar to the bowl and, using your fingers or a muddler, rub the sugar and zest together until the sugar turns a pale yellow color and smells fragrant.

2. Halve the lemons and squeeze 1¼ cups of juice from them. Pour the juice into the sugar mixture, stirring until the sugar dissolves. Strain the mixture into a pitcher and mix in the filtered water. Refrigerate until ready to serve.

3. To serve, pour the lemonade into ice-filled glasses.

Italian Rhubarb-Orange Soda

MAKES: 4 cups

PREP TIME: 8 minutes

COOK TIME: 5 minutes

MAKE-AHEAD: The rhubarb-orange mixture can be made up to 3 days ahead, covered, and refrigerated.

3 blood oranges

3 rhubarb stalks, trimmed and thinly sliced (about 3 cups)

¾ cup sugar

⅓ cup water

Crushed ice

About 4 cups sparkling water, chilled

Take an everyday lunch to gourmet heights with this homemade spin on Italian soda, bubbling with bright, bold natural flavors and colors. A splash of vodka works seamlessly in here too, and you can change things up by swapping out the rhubarb for strawberry, if desired. If blood oranges aren't available, use Valencia oranges instead.

1. Using a Microplane grater, finely grate the zest from the oranges into a medium heavy saucepan.

2. Using a sharp knife, remove all the white pith from the oranges, then cut the flesh into about 1-inch pieces. Add the flesh to the saucepan. Mix in the rhubarb, sugar, and water and bring to a simmer over medium heat, stirring frequently to dissolve the sugar. Simmer, breaking up the fruit with a spoon, for about 5 minutes, or until the rhubarb is completely soft.

3. Push the fruit mixture through a fine strainer into a bowl. Refrigerate until cold.

4. Pour about ⅓ cup of the rhubarb-orange mixture into each of four 8-ounce glasses. Fill the glasses half-full with crushed ice and add enough sparkling water to fill the glasses. Stir and serve immediately.

Fresh Blackberry Cocktail

St-Germain is a French elderflower liquor with distinct, intense floral aromatics, and even the smallest dash gives vibrancy to a summer cocktail. Before you start mixing and muddling, taste the blackberries, as you may need to adjust the amount of sugar. If they are a little tart, use the full 2 teaspoons of sugar, but if they are juicy and sweet, you may want a little less. Master this cocktail, and you've got yourself the perfect summer sundown aperitif or a tasty drink for your Saturday nights.

SERVES: 1

PREP TIME: 5 minutes

3 cups ice cubes

⅓ cup fresh blackberries

2 teaspoons sugar, or to taste

1 tablespoon fresh lime juice

¼ cup silver rum

1 tablespoon St-Germain

¼ cup club soda

1. In a food processor, grind the ice so that it is very finely crushed and fluffy, like shaved ice.

2. Put the blackberries, sugar, and lime juice in a rocks glass and mash with a muddler or a pestle. Stir in the rum, St-Germain, and ½ cup of the crushed ice. Pack more ice into the glass, mounding it well above the rim. Pour the club soda over and serve immediately.

Pineapple-Lime Margaritas

Margarita mix be damned! Tuck this winner in the fridge before your guests arrive so it's ready for the first "Cheers." Don't skip the grated lime zest—it's the key to giving these margaritas good lime flavor. Gold and silver tequila are both great in this recipe—it just depends on your preference. But be sure to use a good-quality tequila.

SERVES: 6

PREP TIME: 10 minutes

MAKE-AHEAD: The pineapple mixture can be made up to 2 days ahead, covered, and refrigerated.

1. In a blender, working in batches, combine the pineapple, lime zest, lime juice, and filtered water and blend until smooth. Strain the mixture through a fine-mesh sieve into an 8-cup measuring cup or pitcher. Stir in the agave, tequila, and Cointreau.

2. Fill six 8-ounce glasses half-full with ice. Pour the margarita mixture over the ice and serve immediately.

1 medium ripe pineapple (4 pounds), peeled, quartered, and cut into large chunks

3 tablespoons finely grated lime zest (from about 4 limes)

¾ cup fresh lime juice (from about 5 limes)

3 cups filtered water

6 tablespoons agave nectar

1½ cups tequila

¼ cup Cointreau

Ice cubes

Spicy and Smoky Bloody Marys

SERVES: 4 to 6

PREP TIME: 5 minutes, plus 20 minutes for soaking the chiles

COOK TIME: 6 minutes

MAKE-AHEAD: The Bloody Mary mixture can be made up to 3 days ahead, covered and refrigerated.

1 dried chipotle chile, stem removed and seeded

1 dried New Mexico chile, stem removed and seeded

4 cups low-sodium tomato juice

½ cup fresh lemon juice (from about 3 lemons)

1 jarred pickled jalapeño, with 2 tablespoons of the brine

1 to 2 tablespoons Tapatío hot sauce or other hot sauce

1 teaspoon Worcestershire sauce

½ teaspoon celery seeds

¾ cup to 1½ cups high-quality vodka

Ice cubes

1 lemon, thinly sliced, for garnish

4 to 6 pieces celery stalks, for garnish

This is a wake-you-up, kick-your-butt-into-gear Bloody Mary. If you would rather wake up a bit slower, scale back on the hot sauce and pickled jalapeño. The dried chipotle chile contributes flavorful smokiness, but if you have trouble finding some, it's OK to omit it—the mix will still be tasty. So good to share with friends over brunch.

1. Heat a small heavy skillet over medium heat. Lay the chiles in the pan and toast them for about 3 minutes per side, or until they are beginning to blacken in spots. Transfer the chiles to a bowl, cover with warm water, and soak the chiles for about 20 minutes, or until they soften.

2. Remove the chiles from the soaking liquid, draining them well, and transfer to a blender. Add the tomato juice, lemon juice, jalapeño and brine, hot sauce, Worcestershire sauce, and celery seeds and blend until completely smooth. Transfer the mixture to a pitcher. Stir in the vodka to taste.

3. Fill tall glasses with ice. Divide the Bloody Mary mixture among the glasses, garnish with the lemon slices and celery, and serve.

GARNISHES

Crunchy celery stalks and tart lemon slices are my favorite classic garnishes for this bold cocktail. But the options are nearly limitless. Try garnishing with small poached shrimp, green olives, pickled onions, or even pickled green beans or asparagus.

Homemade Almond Milk

Homemade almond milk is creamier, nuttier, and more wholesome than any store-bought version. Enjoy it on your morning cereal, in a smoothie, with your favorite cookie, or even in your morning cup of joe.

1. To soak the almonds, in a large container, combine the almonds with enough filtered water to cover them by 4 inches. Cover and refrigerate overnight. Keep an eye on the water level, as the almonds will absorb the water, and add more water as needed to keep them covered.

2. To prepare the almonds, bring a large pot of water to a boil over high heat. Prepare a large bowl of ice water. Drain the almonds and add them to the boiling water, then remove the pot from the heat and let stand for just 25 seconds. Drain the almonds and immediately submerge them in the ice bath. Let the almonds stand until cold, adding more ice if needed to keep the water cold.

3. Drain the almonds. Remove the skins by squeezing one end of each almond so it pops out of the skin and into a bowl.

4. To make the almond milk, line a fine-mesh strainer with a fine-mesh pastry cloth (not cheesecloth; see Note) and set the strainer over a bowl. In a large blender (preferably a high-powered blender), combine 2 cups of the peeled almonds with 2 cups cold filtered water and blend on medium-high speed for about 2 minutes, or until extremely smooth; do not allow the mixture to become warm.

5. Pour the mixture into the strainer and use a ladle to push the milk through the cloth and strainer. To remove the last few drops of milk from the cloth, tightly squeeze the cloth with your hands, allowing the milk to flow through the strainer. Discard the almond solids and return the cloth to the strainer. Repeat blending and straining the remaining almonds and 2 more cups cold filtered water per batch.

6. Pour the almond milk into bottles, cover, and refrigerate for up to 1 week. Shake before serving.

FOR THE PUREST MILK

The key to making a smooth, grit-free almond milk is using a pastry cloth to strain it. Pastry cloths have a much tighter weave than cheesecloth, so only the very purest milk is able to drain through it. Of course, you can find pastry cloths online, but they're also available at most housewares stores, health food stores, and in the kitchen section of some markets.

MAKES: 8 cups

PREP TIME: 1 hour, plus 12 hours for soaking the almonds

COOK TIME: 25 seconds

MAKE-AHEAD: The almonds can be soaked in the water in the refrigerator for up to 3 days; just be sure to refresh the water each day. The almond milk can be made up to 1 week ahead, covered, and refrigerated.

2 pounds unblanched raw almonds
Ice-cold filtered water as needed

Weeknight Belgian Hot Chocolate

MAKES: about 5 cups

PREP TIME: 5 minutes

COOK TIME: 5 minutes

MAKE-AHEAD: The hot chocolate mixture can be made up to 2 days ahead, covered and refrigerated. Rewarm and froth before serving.

4 cups whole or low-fat milk

8 ounces bittersweet chocolate (70% cacao), finely chopped

4 ounces high-quality milk chocolate, finely chopped (about ½ cup)

½ cup Cognac (optional)

¾ cup heavy cream

1 tablespoon powdered sugar

I don't usually make a dessert on a weeknight, but if a chocolate craving creeps up, I often whip up this rich hot cocoa. Linds and I cozy up on the couch, light candles, and sip away. . . . It's a good life. Wrapping my hands around the mug feels so good, and drinking that liquid chocolate is so satisfying all around. Nice with a nip of Cognac or, when I'm trying to be good, I omit the alcohol and whipped cream and use low-fat milk. An immersion blender makes it extra-frothy.

1. In a medium heavy saucepan, stir the milk over medium-high heat until hot. Remove the pan from the heat, add both chocolates, and, using an immersion blender, blend until the chocolate is melted and the mixture is foamy. Blend in the Cognac, if using.

2. In a medium bowl, beat the cream with the powdered sugar until thick and fluffy.

3. Ladle the hot chocolate into your favorite mugs, spoon dollops of the whipped cream on top, and serve immediately.

French Press Coffee

Good coffee is at the very heart of my hometown Melbourne's food and drink culture. I love chatting with the baristas at my local coffee shop, learning about the origins and types of coffee beans they are playing around with. And while sitting down to a spot-on cuppa at one of our hip cafés is a "life's very good right now" moment, I like being able to fix perfect French press coffee at home. Buying the best blend of beans is key, but you've got to back up those beans by carefully monitoring the entire brewing process. Stick to my method below and become the resident barista at your own home.

MAKES: Six 4-ounce cups

PREP TIME: 2 minutes

COOK TIME: 5 minutes

MAKE-AHEAD: Coffee is obviously best enjoyed piping hot, but I sometimes pour leftover French press brew over ice and stir in some milk.

4 cups filtered water

⅓ cup coffee beans

1. Bring the filtered water to a boil in a teakettle or medium saucepan, then remove from the heat and let sit for 30 seconds to 1 minute, or until the temperature of the water is 205°F.

2. Meanwhile, in a coffee grinder, coarsely grind the coffee beans; they should resemble coarse bread crumbs. Transfer to a French press.

3. When the water is at 205°F, pour it over the coffee to almost fill the French press, leaving 1½ inches of space at the top. Let steep for 5 minutes. (Do not cover the press with the plunger at this point.)

4. Add the plunger and slowly plunge the coffee. Serve immediately.

PERFECTION IN EVERY CUP

· I prefer to use a burr grinder for a more even grind, but a blade grinder will work too. Grind the beans just before you brew to make the most of their aromas and oils.

· The water temperature you want is 205°F: hotter or boiling water will burn the coffee; if the temperature is too low, the flavor won't be fully extracted from the coffee.

· I can't overemphasize the importance of a clean French press—make sure there are no coffee grounds stuck in the screen or plunger.

· Let the beans steep for a full 5 minutes to help them "bloom," resulting in maximum flavor.

Acknowledgments

—————

'M UP TO MY THANK-YOUS, which means I've officially penned my sixth cookbook. Six! That seriously gives me the chills. I absolutely love building them from nothing but an idea into the collection of recipes that you're holding today. But the truth is, as you can no doubt tell, I didn't pull this bad boy together on my own. I called on a small group of folks, whom I'm lucky enough to call my friends, to lend a big helping hand.

First up, this book should really be called *Good Food, Good Life* by Curtis Stone and Rochelle Palermo. Rochelle, you never cease to amaze me! You are such a talent and so easily excitable when it comes to food. Your hard work, creativity, passion, and flair have really made this book what it is. This is our third book together and my favorite. You're the best food editor in the business and I am so lucky to work side by side with you.

In the kitchen with us were chefs Matthew Glasser and Andrew Phillips, who rigorously tested these recipes and put up mouthwatering food day after day for the cameras. I don't think Matt will ever look at banana soufflés in the same light again. You can rest assured that the soufflé recipe, and the other 129 recipes, are absolutely spot-on because of their efforts.

Never too far away from the kitchen was fellow Aussie Jessica Foley. I kind of dropped this hot potato in Jess's lap. She had only been in the U.S. for five months, and over a coffee I told her, "You are going to write this book with me." Jess, you have been unbelievable at getting what's in my head (which is sometimes a little disjointed, to say the least) into beautifully crafted sentences. You're a talented writer and I feel so lucky to have you as a part of our little team.

Kate Martindale, you have styled my house, my restaurant, my office, and my books; without you I would be so uncool. We have hit every flea market in L.A. looking for antique plates, linens, old school trinkets, and vases, and I know you have hit a million more without me. Thanks for your beautiful art direction and incredible styling.

A heartfelt thanks to my man, photographer Ray Kachatorian, for capturing the food right at the perfect moment and for ensuring I didn't scrub up too badly in my pics either. It's rare to find a photographer who can take such beautiful food and portrait images, and these that you worked on with the help of Tovin Stith do a phenomenal job of romancing my story.

Vivian Lui, I know I'm a little bit of a control freak when it comes to how my food tastes and looks, so thank you for going above and beyond. The dishes look even more delicious than I had ever envisioned. You're a doll to work with.

Thanks Victoria Andrade, Josefa Gomez, and Paula Castronova for prepping ingredients, shopping, and keeping things nice 'n' tidy throughout the photo-shoot madness. The power of a clear workspace and perfectly peeled, chopped, and washed food cannot be underestimated.

Jodie Gatt (Jet Set), who basically runs my business, is not only my boss on occasion but my best friend. We have worked together for nine years and been friends for way too long. Thanks for keeping us all on track, playing COO, finance manager, publicist, recipe taster, dish washer; you name it and you have done it. I am eternally grateful.

Hannah Randle, you are a breath of fresh air, miracle worker with my calendar, and all that we do. I don't know how you do it, but every single person you deal with at some point tells me how lucky I am to have you, and you know what? They are right.

Brandon Difiglio, Gareth Evans, and Vannessa Garcia, and all of the chefs at Maude, thanks for the inspiration, hard work, and talent you bring to the team. And a special little thanks to my office troops, Danielle Hausner, Rachel McKiernan, and Julia Waldow, for holding down the fort during an especially busy period.

What a pleasure it has been to work on another book with the editorial team at Random House. Thanks to my editor, Pamela Cannon, who played a pivotal role in shaping the theme and style of the book and to the entire art, production, and the publicity teams—both at Random House and the lovely ladies over in NYC, The Brooks Group. You are awesome.

Saving the very best for last here. My gorgeous little family, each of these recipes ties back to memories we have made together in our home. This book, brought to life with our stories and incredible photos of each of you (including you, Emerson, hiding in Mumma's tummy), will forever remind me of this special and fun (and busy!) time in our lives. I'm so excited for our new chapter together as a family of four.

My beautiful Lindsay, thanks for allowing me to stay out late in my restaurant, talk endlessly about food, make a total mess in the kitchen, and drag us all around the world on foodie adventures. Love you more than words can say.

A big cheers to you all, love you loads!

Curtis

Index

About the Author

———

Curtis Stone is the author of six cookbooks, chef-owner of the award winning restaurant Maude in Beverly Hills ("2014's Best New Restaurant" *LA Weekly* and "4 out of 4 stars" *Los Angeles Magazine*), host of Food Network's *Kitchen Inferno,* and regular guest co-host of ABC's *The Chew.* He is also the creator of Kitchen Solutions, a sleek line of cookware sold in retailers worldwide, and writes a bimonthly column for *O, The Oprah Magazine.* Born in Melbourne, Australia, Stone honed his skills in London at Café Royal, under legendary three-star Michelin chef Marco Pierre White, and at Mirabelle and the revered Quo Vadis. He lives in Los Angeles with his wife and two children.

www.curtisstone.com

www.mauderestaurant.com

About the Type

———

This book was set in Centaur, a typeface designed by the American typographer Bruce Rogers in 1929. Rogers adapted Centaur from a fifteenth-century type of Nicholas Jenson (c. 1420–80) and modified it in 1948 for a cutting by the Monotype Corporation.